Poetry is a get-together of emotions. It is a peak inside of human possibility. Dr. Bacon's book shows us the transformative power of this ancient language of love. She shows us how our children, in general, and our black girls, in particular, can come to know and love themselves, and how we can skillfully expedite and support their journey. The curriculum has always been the child, and this life-giving and life-saving study is a dynamic guide for teachers, literacy practitioners, and guardians of *these Black kids.*

Kwame Alexander, #1 New York Times Bestselling Author of *The Door of No Return* Trilogy and *Why Fathers Cry at Night: A Memoir*; Writer/Executive Producer, "The Crossover" on Disney+ & Disney Channel; President, Big Sea Entertainment

The place of poetry in understanding African American adolescent girls in the context of institutional racism is demonstrated through heart and mind. Dr. Jennifer Bacon, an amazing poet and educator, speaks to culture, creativity, and commitment. This commitment beckons us to not only understand, but to act for inclusion, equity, and social justice. The impact of "naming" can be instrumental in damaging or uplifting young people. Bacon's personal narrative and poetry bring multiracial and Black feminism to your door. The "lived experience" of writing poetry is remarkably demonstrated and consistent with the research on expressive writing. On every level of human experience (cognitive, affective, behavioral, and spiritual), this book provides an entry into the power, pain, and promise of poetry to not only African American adolescent girls but to the humanity in all of us. Dr. Bacon truly captures the depth, beauty, and urgency of this process. I find this work to be a model for me to follow my own work in poetry therapy.

Nicholas Mazza, PhD, Professor and Dean Emeritus at the Florida State University, College of Social Work, Tallahassee, FL; Author of *Poetry Therapy; Theory and Practice, 3rd Edition* (2022); Founding (1987) and current editor, *Journal of Poetry Therapy: The Interdisciplinary Journal of Practice, Theory, Research, and Education*

A must-read tour de force, *These Black Kids: Culturally Responsive Poetry and the Lived Experience of African American Adolescent Girls* is truly a masterpiece depicting, as its name implies, the lived experience of a marginalized group languishing on the outskirts of America's mores yet markedly burgeoning within the frame of the American portrait—the most denigrated and least understood cultural group in our society: The African American Adolescent Girl. Not simply a treatise just for Black girls, this artistic production is enlightening to all who will dare delve into their vivacity. Bacon poetically enumerates the throes of life unique to African American adolescent girls and simultaneously celebrates the strength, courage, and resiliency of this unbeknownst ordinary, albeit extraordinary, group impacting our world.

>Nathaniel Granger, Jr., PsyD; Past President, Society for Humanistic Psychology; Editor, Poetry, Healing, and Growth Series, University Professors Press; Co-editor, *Rising Voices: Poems Toward a Social Justice Revolution*

Dr. Bacon's study is an amazing work in drawing out the lived experiences of adolescent girls who were able to name themselves through the poetry writing process she engaged them in through her poetry writing group. The writing of the adolescent girls is so very powerful in displaying what their lived experiences are as African American adolescents struggling for a voice. Dr. Bacon is fast becoming a leading scholar in this area.

>Dr. Francine Hultgren, Professor Emerita & Phenomenological Researcher, University of Maryland, College Park

These Black Kids

Culturally Responsive Poetry and the Lived Experience of African American Adolescent Girls

by
Jennifer Nicole Bacon, PhD

Colorado Springs, CO
www.universityprofessorspress.com

Copyright © 2023

These Black Kids: Culturally Responsive Poetry and the Lived Experience of African American Adolescent Girls
By Jennifer Nicole Bacon

All rights reserved. No portion of this book may be reproduced by any process or technique without the express written consent of the publishers.

ISBN (Hardcover):   978-1-955737-41-8
ISBN (Paperback):   978-1-955737-42-5
ISBN (Ebook):   978-1-955737-43-2

University Professors Press
Colorado Springs, CO
www.universityprofessorspress.com

Cover Image by Sean Carney
Back Cover Photo by Sofia Drobinskayas
Cover Design by Laura Ross

Dedication

Past~ This book is dedicated to the wisdom of the foremothers and ancestors and to the Black women on whose shoulders we stand.
Present~ To "These Black Kids" whose courage, brilliance, and voices inspired this work.
Future~ To the generation of writers to come.

***

For my parents and their love, legacy, wisdom, and guidance. Your love and inspiration continue to live on inside me.
For my husband and fortress and our sacred life journey together.
For the most beautiful and brightest light of my life, my daughter.
For my sister, who inspired the grounding for this exploration and journey into sisterhood and solidarity.
For my beloved soul-friends who walk this path beside me.

Table of Contents

Acknowledgments		i
Foreword *by Will Alexander*		iii
Introduction		v
Section One	These Black Kids	1
Section Two	The Poetic Beginning: Uncovering Muted Voices	10
Section Three	Looking for Lost Black Girls	19
Section Four	Poetry: The Creation of Selves	25
Section Five	What African American Adolescent Girls Do	29
Section Six	Becoming the Poetic Eight	52
Section Seven	My Real Name	79
Section Eight	Poetic Love	101
Section Nine	Honoring the Divine	133
Section Ten	The Pedagogy of Poetry	139
References		167
Index		173
Author Bio		175

Acknowledgments

My deepest gratitude and appreciation for the genuine support, encouragement of, commitment to, and enthusiasm for this research and writing journey to "Blue," Dr. Francine Hultgren, "the Poetic Eight," Dr. Shanna Smith, RA Heléne Van den Berg, Mr. Will Alexander, Dr. Regina Young, Dr. Omari Daniel, Mr. Solomon Comissiong, Dr. Renetta Tull, Dr. Xochitl Vallejos, Dr. Louis Hoffman, Dr. Nicholas Mazza, Mr. Kwame Alexander, Ms. Denise Vega, Rev. Dr. Doris McGuffey, and Dr. Susan Burggraf.

My sincerest gratitude and appreciation for such instrumental support by University Professors Press, The National Association for Poetry Therapy, Black Women Writing, The Believe Scholarship, Book-in-A-Day Writing Fellowship, PROMISE, Poetry Alive: Poetry Therapy Grant Award, Pursue a Dream: Chris Mazza Poetry Therapy Grant Award, SisterMentors, the Diversity and Inclusion Committee of Naropa University, the Summer Writing Program, and Fielding Graduate University.

Foreword

Jennifer Bacon's *These Black Kids* soars beyond its architectural brilliance, enlightening by its ascent the instructor–student relationship. In essence, it is a seminal primer for educators concerned with conveying poetry as an instrument for interior awakening. It shows in concrete fashion learning through lingual ignition. Bacon reminds us (through various examples) that verbal doors can open for the student onto an inner vastness where fertility is sustained by means of one's intrinsic intelligence. Thus, Bacon's *Writing in Solidarity* remains a trenchant guide for honing verbal capability sans scholarly super-imposition. Poetic exploration in this context is naturally understood as uncontaminated expression, simultaneous as it is with one's living arc. It produces a momentum not unlike the electricity that is insight. As philosopher, writer, and speaker Siddu Krishnamurti has pointed out, insight kindles healing in the brain. So, for contemporary urban adolescents condensed by the pressures and counter-pressures of the present era, the healing broached by this "Guide" is nothing other than a psychic flambeau that illuminates the path to inner liberty, providing the spirit with a healthy attitude toward living.

    Will Alexander
    Poet, Visual Artist, Essayist, Novelist, Playwright, and
    Philosopher; Author of *Towards the Primeval Lightning Field*;
    Asia & Haiti; *Exobiology as Goddess*

Introduction

This book, which is based on my dissertation research, "Culturally Responsive Poetry: The Lived Experience of African American Adolescent Girl Poets," has developed alongside my own poetic and life journey. Culturally responsive poetry is the unearthing of African American adolescents' self-definition through a process of naming (to call forth their own names and multiple identities). It involves poetry writing as both individual and collective efforts by and for African American adolescent girls as a bold and passionate declaration of self-identity. The process of creating culturally responsive poetry for African American adolescent girls becomes a deeply meaningful recognition and expression of multiple identities that include race, gender, age, class, and location. Moreover, embedded in the fabric of culturally responsive poetry is the voice of resistance. The voices of resistance and identity that are revealed in culturally responsive poetry are connected theoretically throughout Black feminism, multiracial feminism, and intersectionality. The result is a form of writing that calls for the merger of scholarship with creative and poetic expression.

The journey of African American adolescent girl poets uncovering the power to name themselves as a phenomenon reflects the beauty and angst of self-discovery, identity, and self-definition. Phenomenology unfolds the poets' lived experiences, deepening the meaning of each writing experience, as the process reflects not only the essence and meaning of the poems but the essence of the poet. Phenomenology as a practice and methodology surrenders to lived experiences (the world as we immediately experience it rather than conceptualize it) through a process that is as reflexive and profound as poetry writing itself. This research, then, can be seen as a poetic rendering of the poetry writing experiences of African American adolescent girl poets in order to uncover their multiple identities (Bacon, 2009, pp. ii–iii).

My phenomenological research study is further grounded in Black feminism and multiracial feminism and provides a diversity of adolescent girls' voices. The aim of this book is to provide a deepened understanding and awareness of the multiple identities of African American adolescent girls and women, and the refinement of research methods on race, gender, class, and age. This work forges a path for underrepresented groups (primarily African Americans, girls/women, and youth with exceptionalities) in order for them to display multiple identities and receive recognition for their creative writing and expression (Bacon, 2009).

As anti-Black racism has become more visible to mainstream society as a result of televised acts of racial violence in contemporary times, so have the activism and voices of youth who have directed society to confront its practices, patterns, systems, microaggressions, and outright acts of rage and violence. Liberatory practices require not only critical praxis in terms of understanding the significance of intersectionality but the significance of social justice and activism through the engagement of practice by those who embody it.

From beyond the gaze and oppression of white culture is an expression of hope and a self-defined identity/naming. *These Black Kids* explores race, gender, school, culture, and relationships. Other components include self-identity, self-image, and empowerment for adolescent girls. In addition, the cultural, social, individual, and collective nature and process of writing in solidarity provide experiences of interacting reflectively with ideas that pertain to the girls' lives.

In my current work as a professor in education, creative writing, human development, and sacred activism, I revisit the poetry of my participants, who were often in high school at the time. Teaching middle and high school in many ways has most shaped my path as a university professor, mentor, and writer. Moreover, it has inspired my path as a mother and as a spiritual human being.

As adults, we often look back to remember in gratitude our most inspirational teachers from our childhoods. The teachers that believed in us even during the times that we did not believe in ourselves. Who nurtured our voices, helped us recognize and express our gifts, made us want to come to class or to school at all. They may have shaped our chosen professions or helped us develop courage to try different paths.

As a teacher/educator who will be entering my 24th year of teaching, from preschool-aged children through graduate school, I look back on my educational journey to recognize not only the teachers (the most influential teacher being my own mother) and mentors who inspired me but also my students. The students whom I have never forgotten over the years, whose stories still inspire courage, whose paths fortified my dedication to the field of education and commitment to underserved communities, silenced voices, and educational equity and activism. Three of those students are "Keisha," "Mishaps," and "Blue" (all are pseudonyms used with permission, with two chosen as pen names by the student participants themselves. I also note that different pseudonyms have been used for "Keisha" in varying publications).

Section One

These Black Kids

These **Black Kids**
What is the lived experience of writing poetry for African American adolescent girls to uncover the power to name who they really are? This section explores this phenomenon more deeply, turning to a variety of sources and writings for this uncovering and naming. Naming has the power to define you. It can create who you are and define who you are not. As my students seek to uncover who they really are, I seek to unfold the process of who they are not. My students are not "These Black Kids" as defined by others.

These Black Kids

This poem is for these Black kids who laugh with their mouths open and uncovered
This poem is for these Black kids who speak not only with their mouths but also with their necks (wiggling), eyes (rolling), and hips (swiveling)
It's for the Black kids whom the sub, in the regular teacher's absence, calls "lazy, stupid, complainers"
This poem is for these Black kids who listen when we are not looking

    Who cherish every A and gold star they ever earned
    Who call out without their hands raised – but always have the right answer
Who have been scribbling poems of poverty on toilet paper and having babies at 14 as we "teach" them the rhyme scheme of ABAB

    This poem is for Rachel who sleeps drooling on the desk for 50 minutes...

1. These Black Kids

after taking care of a crying baby sister all night
because Mama didn't come
home–
again –

Rachel who tried to go to the store for milk
only to be chased away for the crime of looking like a
kid who may have shoplifted yesterday
"I don't know – they all look alike anyway."

This poem is for these Black kids who spent the night being
stalked by the police...
for standing outside & together - trying to explain the projects
have no AC and the suffocating heat is too much for young
souls to sleep

This poem is for Tyrone who spent the morning
picking up bottles and vials after
daddy's "party" –

For Tyrone with stained clothes, and stale breath,
bread and butter smeared homework,
who crouched for hours in the under-sized closet
studying by flashlight in the only place where there's
a little bit of quiet and daddy's hands don't roam
after the "guests" are gone.

This poem is for those Black kids who didn't make it to the
closet last night... And whose neighbors turned up the
television to drown out their muffled screams and cries
instead of calling the police
This poem is for Tyesha who limps in quietly after the bell
rings and struggles to sit sideways to protect the sliced flesh
on her backside from one more beating—infraction
unknown
This poem is for the tight-lipped, baby, warriors who defiantly
hold the "private business" of "family affairs"

CPS never comes:
Can't find/prove anything
Too scared.

> Pupil Personnel Workers explain procedures instead of making home visits unless "absolutely necessary"
> "Oh, and teacher referrals aren't accepted—only administration can make that call."

And prune-faced substitutes hiss hatefully, "why can't these Black kids behave?!"
(Bacon, 2009, pp. 36–37; Bacon, 2011b, pp. 2–3)

I was co-teaching in an inclusion (general education and special education) English class in a diverse suburban public secondary school at the time I wrote "These Black Kids." In spite of the school's racial and ethnic diversity, my special education students were predominantly Black children from urban areas and/or were from low-income families. Although inclusion classes were designed to incorporate special education students in the general education setting, the majority of my ninth grade Black special education children seemed to be "tracked" into one English classroom.

I wrote the poem in response to actual events that had occurred throughout my teaching career as well as a specific incident in which a substitute teacher referred to the Black children in my class as "lazy," "stupid," "animals." On this particular day, the substitute teacher conducted the class along with the general education teacher and the general education teacher's student-teacher. Our class was always lively, and the children often verbally expressive and animated. Many of our students, unbeknownst to the substitute, had endured traumatic experiences at some point in their lives such as abandonment by loved ones through death or temporary or permanent desertion; poverty; physical or sexual abuse by adults or boyfriends (some resulting in pregnancy); and/or previous discrimination and marginalization based on their race, class, gender, and disability (Bacon, 2009, 2011b).

However, my students frequently expressed a zeal for life, enthusiasm for learning, debates, and discussions. Although the children called out frequently during class or some, like many children, may have experienced difficulty remaining in their seats, their answers were almost always correct, and they remained actively and verbally engaged in the lessons. However, rather than naming the students resilient, persistent, creative, or survivors, the substitute chose to "name" the Black children "loud," "stupid," and "lazy," and further decided they "could not behave or learn." Although both the general education teacher and the student-teacher reported the incident to me, and I took immediate action, neither of the other teachers voiced their dissatisfaction, concerns, or opinions to anyone else but me (not even to the substitute teacher).

It is my belief and experience that this was not the first or last time that Black students, particularly in special education, would be subjected to this type of discrimination in and out of the classroom and have their voices silenced. Therefore, I felt it was imperative to create opportunities for my students to express themselves, tell their stories, determine their own identities, and receive positive affirmation of their culture(s). Based on many of my students' interests, I determined that African American adolescents could create this opportunity through reading and writing poetry (Bacon, 2009, 2011b, 2016, 2017).

The Poetic Journey
The poetic journey began after I transferred from a suburban southern school to an urban/suburban school in a neighboring state. This journey was much different. The drive to the school building was long and tedious in the early morning. I would awaken in the dark and travel in its despair to my destination. Someone once commented that it must be beautiful to drive into the sunrise. It was not. The sun rose behind me most of the journey and never spread her arms across the length of the sky, and when the road would twist in her direction, I was reminded of her fury. It was a blinding scorching turmoil that always made you want to shut your eyes tightly, knowing that if you looked at it directly it would cost you your sight (Bacon, 2009).

A Joyless Place: Legacies Lost

Bachelard (1994) quotes Noel Arnaud in *The Poetics of Space*: "I am the space where I am" (p. 14). Where I am is dank and cold. The building does not hold warmth in the winter or cold in the summer. It does not hold sunshine, for there are no windows. It does not hold joy. The walls are sterile slabs of bricks that resemble a prison. The institution was designed with freedom in mind and, therefore, allows for open spaces, classrooms without walls. However, the open spaces allow the sound of unrest to sweep through, but the air does not. The air smells stale and used. Toxins are breathed out with nothing clean or new brought in. A lingering pain cloaks the rooms like a musty, wet blanket designed for putting out fires that still smolder undetected (Bacon, 2009, 2011b).

We are too close together. The dirty desks and broken chairs are crammed upon one another. Each student's body, small as a sixth grader and large as an eighth grader, has been stuffed into those desks at one point in time. We cannot all fit into this closet, with soiled carpet, slanting bookshelves, and droppings of whatever has come to darken our door the night before. Occasionally, one who is cumbersome in size sits uncomfortably with their fat squishing from outside the chair. There is my sweet Tommy who has a glandular problem. His face is that of an angel; he keeps his smile plastered to his gentle brown cheeks, as the other children slide their desks away and hold their noses. His mother forgot his Depends diapers this morning, and the urine leaks quietly undetected until it hits the air. I get up unsteadily from my own squishy chair to rush to his aid. The back from the vomit-colored-orange-upholstered chair is missing. It should have been discarded at a 1970s garage sale.

The substitute's obesity broke the chair's back. It is a metaphor for all of us too large to be caged in this stifling space. We are like Great Danes in the pound in cages made for Chihuahuas. Maybe they think we will be subdued, and maybe some of us do shrink in stature to accommodate the low roofs, limits, and low expectations of who and what we really are. Maybe we are, indeed, our space.

I cannot protect them from the mice and roaches that will lurk throughout the building once we leave, if we are lucky. I cannot protect them from the teachers who call them animals and say they cannot learn. I cannot protect them from viewing the girl raped in the neighborhood who ran naked into the street. I cannot protect them from being duct taped to the clothes dryer and beaten until it is too late and the damage is done. I cannot protect them from the knowledge that their fathers were killed in a drug deal gone wrong, or their mothers' belt that will not be spared when she gets home after working two jobs and going to night school and has nothing left to give.

I cannot protect them on the bus when the child with autism is forced to perform oral sex by two other young, misguided special education boys whom we had repeatedly pushed to have placed in a program for "emotionally and behaviorally disordered" children prior to the rape. And I cannot protect them in the bathroom when one child follows the other in and molests him. The administration says it is a case of standing too close together at the urinals, and the paperwork is "accidentally" discarded. And on many days, I feel I cannot protect them from one another, even in my classroom when desks begin to fly across the room in frustration and anger (Bacon, 2009, 2011b).

At the Intersections

Social locations of race, class, ethnicity, gender, ability, sexual orientation, and geographic location, among others, make up the major forms of oppression in the United States by creating an unjust situation where one group systematically denies another group access to resources in society. "Without the power to influence the purpose and direction of our collective experience, without the power to influence our culture from within, we are increasingly immobilized" (Collins, 2000, p. 88). This systematic oppression may lead to further alienation from a truly self-defined identity and a connection to other students and cultural legacies.

For the African American adolescent girls in my book, exploring the intersections of race and gender through writing and a collaborative process of sharing appear to be critical components in acquiring knowledge and a sense of self. Furthermore, poetry writing as a cultural practice may be rendered through and by community, humanity, and pedagogical intention (Beech, 1999; Bacon, 2009). Poetry writing for healing, naming, growth, discovery, and community remain the main focus of this book; however, theoretical approaches to understanding, acknowledging, and revealing the lived experience of African American adolescent girls have deeply influenced my writing through the lens and framework of multiracial feminism, Black feminism, and intersectionality.

Multiracial feminism and Black feminism have provided the framework in this research to make narratives and counter-narratives more explicitly audible academically, intellectually, creatively, and socially. Multiracial feminism and Black feminism as theoretical frameworks also augment the research of Tolman (1994, 1996) on urban girls, specifically as they unpack and challenge myths and stereotypes about African American women and girls, their experiences, sexuality, and poetic expression.

Racial disparities must be confronted and placed at the forefront in presenting counter-stories to misinterpretations of experiences. Understanding counter-narratives is also shaped by intersectionality. Intersectionality reveals the complexity of human experiences, which is rarely shaped by one factor or facet of identity (Collins & Bilge, 2016). These counter-stories provide liberation from multiple hierarchies based on race, gender, class, and location. This is especially important in sharing the poetry and writings of African American girls in this book in order not to present a fragmented portrayal of the girls' experiences but a holistic one.

When the individual process of naming through poetry writing is connected with multiracial feminism and Black feminism, will it create a collective experience of naming for the poets? What new understandings might be uncovered for African American adolescent girls if the lenses of Black feminism and multiracial feminism are used to interpret their narrative structures? Black feminism, in this study, primarily is explored through the lens of Black feminist thought and the works of Patricia Hill Collins (2000). Black feminist thought is constructed in such a way as to lend action to Black feminist theory in academia. Black feminist thought also provides the venue and necessary recognition, sense of self, and collective sense of "knowing" to ignite the inaudible voice, heightening it into a high-pitched scream demanding to be heard. And while many traditional theories are created, maintained, or discussed within the post-secondary setting, Black feminist thought acknowledges a broad spectrum of locations and outlets, including poetry and journal writing, independently and through community organizations.

Moreover, Black feminist thought, while empowering African American adolescent girls to seek and define their own identities, simultaneously emphasizes collaboration and cooperation for the benefit of a collective voice and experience (Collins, 2000). Defining an identity also includes the acknowledgement of self-defined sexuality and expression, as well as the relentless struggle to eradicate violence (domestic, societal, and institutional) and sexual abuse and exploitation. "To be able to express the range of one's voice to express the totality of self" while negotiating and reconciling "internally defined images of self as African American women (and girls) without objectification as the Other" is primary (Collins, 2000, p. 99). Black feminism is further grounded in this research by the work of activist, scholar, and attorney Kimberlé Crenshaw, who created the term intersectionality in 1989. Crenshaw's work underscored the critical impact of the intersections of race and gender for Black/African American women (Crenshaw, 2016; Love, 2019).

Through the use of Black feminism and intersectionality, I seek to illuminate the experiences of the adolescent girl participants as they engage in a poetic rendering of their experiences. Black women scholars, researchers, activists, and writers have paved a way for resistance, justice, community, self-expression, and voice as they help provide a basis for counter-narratives. Furthermore, I have chosen to weave Black feminism and intersectionality throughout my exploration of the phenomenon—thus providing a connection between the individual and collective spirit and voices of Black women and adolescent girls brought forth through their poetry and scholarship as well as my own. I instinctively turn toward phenomenology as I ponder the lived experience of writing poetry for African American adolescent girls as they uncover the power to name who they really are.

Phenomenology allows this process to unfold through an in-depth, interpretative exploration and conversation of the meaning of human experience through encounters, deep readings, reflection, and revelation (Garran, 2004). Phenomenology is the place where analysis and philosophy surrender to poetic expression. Poetic connections and distinctions are revealed through lived experience, which is immediate and naturally reflexive, creating the sensation of an unaware awareness. Dilthey (as cited in van Manen, 2003) suggests that "Lived experience is to the soul what breath is to the body" (p. 36). Lived experience is also the critical beginning and ending point of my phenomenological study and research.

A phenomenological study of poetic renderings allows me to journey deeply enough into poetic imagination and truth(s) to describe the ways in which adolescent girls who reside between the borders of girlhood and womanhood are connected to one another, not only by race and gender but their being/essence and experience. Poetic expression allows each writer to open up first to herself and then to one another. Yet, each of their poetic renderings remain so distinctive that they may be perceived as the "other," even within the same poetry group. Although my role as a scholar and researcher requires that I provide some interpretation and "narration" of participants' writing and discussions, it is my goal to preserve the authenticity of the poets' words, feelings, or discussions in their most original form possible. I am called by the phenomenological question, "What is the lived experience of writing poetry to uncover the power for African American adolescent girls to name who they really are?"

Creatively and culturally, poetic discourse in the African American community is saturated by rich language, storytelling, metaphors, meaningful conversation, and political and social commentaries. Poetry may be heard, shared, and spoken in a voice that reflects a cultural context and exchange of everyday language. There is a particular power in poetic language and communication shared through the written word. Reading and sharing poetry are a necessity for many poets who have created a culture that embodies the "language of life" and "living words" (Sundiata & Troupe, as cited in Moyers, 1995; Bacon, 2009, 2011b, 2016).

Poetry writing is, as shared by poets, a source of illumination, providing the possibility of essential expression for thoughts and feelings. Poetry, as a language, can be used in such a way as to make the poetry itself a part of the writer's everyday cultural experience. It is so powerful a medium that it does not only represent an experience, but it *is experienced*, allowing poems to become "living words" (Sundiata, as cited in Moyers, 1995, p. 394).

Words live and breathe their existence from your heart to your listeners. Living texts are full of passion, motion, and response and rhythm to feelings, rather than words that remain dry and flat on a page. This creation of living words or living texts is one of the many cultural experiences and ways of knowing by the community/collective of African American poetic voices.

Poetry as a "living word" situates the writing experience in a cultural space, as well as a space of discourse, relationships, and humanity. Students have found that by sharing these experiences and feelings through poetry they are not alone. This is of particular importance, as it is not only silence that keeps poets subdued but isolation.

This begins my call to "These Black Kids."

Section Two

The Poetic Beginning: Uncovering Muted Voices

"You don't know me, unless you know how hard I try not to cry!"

Keisha[1] is a high school junior whose voice and presence fills the entire room with its volume and exuberance. And while she appears to speak freely and with ease, her authentic voice is often muted. Keisha, like many adolescent girls, has a voice that has been muted by the spaces where her words wither into inaudible noises, fall upon "unlistening ears," or are strangled into silence. Yet her voice, along with the emergence of her true identity, seems to be unearthed when she writes poetry.

Keisha wrote "You Don't Know Me" in one of our poetry group sessions. At the time she was in a tumultuous relationship with a boy who off and on attended another high school in between brief stints in jail for the sale of narcotics. I first became aware of Keisha's writing in our inclusion (special education and general education) ninth grade English class. While other students were writing flowery love poems or poems that resembled nursery rhymes, Keisha was writing poems about teenage violence, infidelity, and sexual encounters with a nineteen-year-old boyfriend. Her experiences chronicled in her poetry exposed a tension between violence, sexual desire, and dangerous exploitation. Although her poetic "confessions" were unnerving at times, there was a vulnerability and truth that could only be uttered through the words on the page.

Keisha's poetry was forceful and unapologetic, yet there seemed to be questions left unanswered in her poetry as she struggled with her desire to be loved as she writes, "Because I thought I was in love, looking at the cards I was dealt." Keisha was also in a struggle to determine her identity. As Keisha's exploration through poetry

---

[1] A pseudonym that has been updated from a previously used pseudonym.

continued, she would chronicle her sexual experiences: the unfaithful nineteen-year-old boyfriend in ninth grade, the sexual assault by a classmate, the first unwanted pregnancy in tenth grade, and the second unwanted pregnancy in eleventh grade. Keisha rarely spoke of the death of her stepmother or her two cousins, and only referenced it once in her poetry. However, questions about love, identity, visibility, and sexuality were themes that surfaced throughout her writing. Uncovering her muted voice, thoughts, and experiences may emerge for Keisha, and other poets, not only through their personal process of poetic expression but through the voices of other writers. There is a pressing need to resist the call to fragment or silence their multiple identities (Bacon, 2009, 2011b, 2017).

Keisha's essence is shared through her lived experience as the memories embedded in her soul leap out at the reader when she writes and reads her poetry. Yet, the conviction with which Keisha writes and reads her poetry is conspicuously missing when she responds during our discussions to the content of her poems. During our discussions, Keisha describes the events of her life revealed in "You Don't Know Me" as if she were rattling off items on a grocery list. Although Keisha does not utter words of anguish in our discussion about the rape, her recent abortion, or her boyfriend cheating, the poem "Abortion Cycle #1," written by Ntozake Shange in *For Colored Girls who have Considered Suicide When the Rainbow is Enuf* seems to seep the unspoken emotion that is missing when Keisha discloses the events: "metal horses gnawin my womb dead mice fall from my mouth...this hurts this hurts me" (Shange, 1977, p. 22).

When Keisha speaks of just coming out of the hospital, showing the places on her arm where she received the IV, it is in a monotone voice. She speaks of her "operation." And she shares that the would-be-father is back in jail. Keisha also shares that she has taken the advice of her mother and me to get tested after learning that he cheated (like the boyfriend in ninth grade). She's contracted something, but it's not HIV, and it can be "fixed" like the "other situation" (the pregnancy). She understands what we discussed in our last poetry group meeting, and she knows that he is at least the third boy to hurt her, "place her in harm's way," or cheat on her. She softly declares that she will "leave him alone" eventually. Keisha knows she deserves better, but he depends on her and recognizes that she is the best thing that has happened to him. His mother even agrees. The monotone voice in which Keisha speaks is deafening. Her pain seeps through the empty spaces and pregnant pauses with the force of a poisonous gas leaking from a faulty stove in the quiet of the night (Bacon, 2009). The final echo of Shange's (1977) poem pierces the silence: "this hurts me..." (p. 22).

Keisha Unknown

Keisha is a regular participant in the poetry group. She is bright, creative, passionate, and animated. Keisha is college bound, hardworking, determined, and driven. She is viewed as an expert in writing and a leader in the poetry group. Yet Keisha, without poetry, seems to have a barely audible voice in expressing her own identity. She is like many girls who reach adolescence and find their sexuality, identity and need for relationships heightened, along with their feelings of vulnerability and disempowerment (Bacon, 2009; Tolman, 1994).

Keisha's vulnerability and disempowerment are revealed as she shares her experiences after being raped. Her desperate attempts at being heard are met with accusations of being a "liar" and a "slut." She is labeled not only by boys but by girls who previously claimed to be her friends. Keisha struggles to reconcile her relationships and her identity, attempting to negotiate feelings of love, confusion, and pain. Yet questions linger about her identity, other people's perceptions of her, society's expectations, and what she will be named. Keisha's fears are illuminated in Shange's poem "Latent Rapists," which exposes another violent silencing of the female spirit through the isolation and scrutiny she is forced to endure. Shange's poem illuminates the disbelief and shame placed on victims through the belief that a rapist must only be a stranger to be considered a "legitimate" violation (Shange, 1977, p. 17).

Silent Bodies

If sexual experiences become saturated with fear, pain, or false accusations of provoking victimization, can girls reclaim their voices and their bodies? Tolman (1994, p. 324) reports that for many adolescent girls, their bodies, much like their voices, become silent. "Silent bodies" are girls who disappear during sex, become confused, or perform because it is expected. They experience being denigrated and controlled through physical or sexual abuse. If abuse is absent in the relationship, desire and arousal still remain laced with fear, fear not only of physical danger but of tarnished reputations, reinforcement of stereotypes, internalized oppression, and the pressure to silence their own bodies from enjoyment. Their total beings (voices, minds, bodies) exist without sound. Fear, pain, and danger are embedded in sexual experiences. What does it mean to live in "silenced" bodies? If girls are afraid of what their bodies are labeled, who do they become when draped in such shame?

For African American adolescent girls, the dichotomy and impact of externally controlled images seem to be even more evident as African American girls report a more pronounced fear of being labeled and fear of sexual desire (Tolman, 1996). However, for "the urban girl" even the "luxury" of a dichotomy is absent. The urban girl is portrayed as a stereotypical, one-dimensional caricature of the adolescent girl and is believed to be amoral or out of control. She is believed to be the embodiment of female adolescent sexuality, representing all that is not only "bad" but "abnormal" (Bacon, 2009, 2011b; Tolman, 1996).

In addition to age and gender, the urban girl also forces us to confront disparity in race and class as she, in spite of statistics and narratives that reveal the pronounced sexual activity of White and suburban girls, is almost always depicted as Black (or Latina) and poor (Tolman, 1996). As a researcher, I am cognizant of the stereotypes, distortions, and caricatures of urban girls, and I actively seek to eliminate and redefine pre-conceived notions and assumptions. However, it is of even greater importance in this phenomenological study that the girls (all of whom are African Americans, some originally from urban areas geographically, and from low-income as well as middle- to upper-income, families) ultimately define, name, and identify themselves. The "urban girl" is forced to confront external images, negative stereotypes, and myths about her identity as the embodiment of immorality and inappropriate sexuality, as well as the misinterpretation and distortion of her experiences. It appears even more critical that she be provided the opportunity to write her experiences, share her own voice, and tell her own truths to uncover the power to name herself.

Writing and reading poetry allow a space for Keisha (who has been labeled an urban girl by others) and other adolescent girl participants to reveal emotional pain and turmoil while writing for empowerment and strength. Reflecting on poems enriches this space to consider the impact of personal experiences, the magnitude of internal and external conflicts, and the ways in which to elicit support. Moreover, reading poems offers a way in which adolescent girls can find their voices outside of externally defined roles or identities. These possibilities are revealed as I continue with Keisha's poetry (Bacon, 2009, 2011b):

> You may think you know me because of my past. Think because of my looks you can predict my future.

The raw places revealed in Keisha's poems echo the experiences shared in Tolman's study. Each girl and woman questions in their stories and their writing "Who will hear their voices through the confusion, façade, and transformation from girl to woman?" Who will penetrate the "outer shell...that is shown to be me?" And for the "urban girl" and the Black woman, the poetry that has been shared dares the reader to know them and embrace them in such a way as to hold them so close to their own hearts that they become part of the reader's own heartbeat.

Songwriter, jazz singer, actress, and civil rights activist Abbey Lincoln writes, "Who will Revere the Black Woman" (1966). She further magnifies this call as she chronicles: "She [the Black woman] has been used as the white man's sexual outhouse." And "Raped and denied the right to cry out in her pain she has been named the culprit and called... amoral."

Lincoln's voice is further amplified in her piece "To Whom Will She Cry Rape" (2005), which floods the pages with the experiences of the metaphorical rape of the Black woman's and girl's psyche. Words are written about the violation of the Black woman's innocence and her soul that hemorrhages with grief, but also the hope of redemption. Keisha's call resembles that of Lincoln's call in her writing as "To Whom Will She Cry Rape" is not only centered upon a physical assault but an emotional one.

This emotional assault so violently shatters the spirit of the African American adolescent girl that it leaves her emotionally desolate and subdued (Bacon, 2009). Keisha's poem, like Lincoln's piece, resides in those quiet spaces where she remains violated and maligned as long as she remains unheard. The poet, along with the listener who hears her cry through her writing, must confront each layer of stereotypes, caricatures, and exploitation to validate the writer's indignation and rectify her debasement in order to protect her identity as much as her innocence. The poet, and the listener, must look past the layers of adolescence, femininity, myths about race, labels, definitions by others, conformity, and untruths to make visible what goes unseen.

Unmuted: Voicing the Experience

> If you wanted to know about me you would have to look really deep... Understand the real me...
> ~ Keisha

Poetry allows the writer to share her own vulnerable experiences such as bouts of depression or domestic violence that can be connected to the lived experiences of others. The poetic process allows for the possibility of uncovering the power for the girl poet to name herself in spite of an external, as well as sometimes internal, need to silence her voice and hide her identity (ies) or find an escape by helping others, frequently males, to find their power while denying her own.

Rather than the girl and women poets escaping into wonder, many African American adolescent girls and women were dragged into the wilderness emotionally, psychically, and physically. Through the poetry shared, an overpowering awareness was revealed that Black girls and women individually and collectively are gone. They are vanishing into the wilderness to perish through voicelessness and isolation. Listening to the writer's poetry enables us to not only hear her, but for her to hear herself. Conversely, when cries fall on deaf ears and the voices of those considered to be the "Other" are further pushed to the margins by our own need to dominate, feel powerful or maintain the status quo, we not only fail to ease human suffering but our collective deafness actually becomes responsible for creating suffering (Bacon, 2009; Levin, 1989). This suffering resembles being dragged out into the wilderness alone.

> Wilderness: Alone
>   dragged out into the death of night
>   where the only sounds are the screams of fear
> mixed with the laughter of another far enough away
> that her voice cannot be reached
> close enough to me that I know somewhere in the darkness
> there is a presence of another
> another who sees his hands grasping at me
> wrapping themselves around my neck pulling me deeper
> into the darkness
>
> Sharpness of his voice
> Slicing cutting digging at what is numb in my soul

> Thrust out to be swallowed by the wilderness
>
> abandoned
> doors shut behind me
> openings out of the darkness fastened
> instead raw openings leak unsealed terror
>
> howls of the wilderness
> daring me to find my way home
> (Bacon, 2009, pp. 21–22)

As I reflect on the wilderness alone, I think back to a student who did not yet uncover her true name or identity before she was cast out to find her way home alone. After participating in the poetry group for almost a year, she stops attending. Shortly after she stops attending the poetry group, she stops attending classes. Shortly after she stops attending classes, she withdraws from school.

My student withdrew from school to move out of the state after being cast out of her house by her mother. Her mother is tired, raising her and her two young siblings alone and recently starting a new job. What's more, her mother expresses that she doesn't need her anymore. She is the girl/woman into whom other adolescent girl students are beginning to emerge. My student is now eighteen and in the eleventh grade, having been retained twice. Her mother wants her to set an example for her younger siblings and to serve as a role model, but instead her mother defines her as disrespectful and defiant.

I think back to high school and my own desire to define myself and be thought of as a grown woman. Coming of age always seems to involve some sort of wrestling for "power" between mothers and daughters. I remember my mother in exasperation declaring one day, "There will only be one woman to a house and if you feel that you are that woman it is time to get your own house." Yet my student's mother's declaration was not an empty gesture or reminder of boundaries, or the reality of adolescent limitations versus authentic womanhood. Her mother defined her as a woman who should be self-sufficient and cast her out.

My student's mother and I talked for over an hour on the phone. Her mother is adamant that the school has falsely identified her as having an emotional and behavioral disorder and defines her daughter's behavior simply as an "attitude problem." It, according to her mother, is time for her to step up to the plate and become strong, resourceful, resilient, and independent. All of these things my student must learn and do on her own because she is now a woman. But what neither of us speak, question, or clarify is the fact that she seems to be expecting her daughter to do these things at the young age of eighteen because she is a Black woman, and what is more, a Black urban woman (Bacon, 2009).

Monique W. Morris, scholar and author *of Pushout: The Criminalization of Black Girls in School,* documents the branding, discrimination, marginalization, and mislabeling of Black girls in schools based on the intersections of race and gender. Such mislabeling includes categorizing Black girls as "defiant." Morris further chronicles what she refers to as "age compression," in which Black girls are denied their girlhood and are forced by society to be seen as women rather than girls and are subjected to the stereotypes that accompany being labeled as Black women (Morris, as cited in Love, 2019).

However, there seems to be some recognition of the limitations of my student's mother's request, and the school's assessment, and arrangements have been made for my student to live with her best friend and her family. As the details of the conversation swirl around in my head, I become aware of the words, "best friend." Does she have a female best friend? I am struck by the fact that she has a best friend, as much as I am struck by the fact that she has been experiencing such turmoil in the relationship with her mother. My student has never written poems about her mother or their relationship or even referenced her, as the other girls have done in conversations in the poetry group. My student has never mentioned a best friend or any female friends. In English class, I rarely, if ever, see her interact with anyone who is not a male, and those interactions appear limited as well.

Upon further reflection, I realize my student has never written about anything but her boyfriend, and while she writes about him, she often is reluctant to have a conversation about her writing. I ponder what these unspoken or barely existent relationships with other girls and women will mean for my student whose lived experience seems to be unfolding like a Toni Morrison novel. I think about what it means for her to be put "outside" of her house by her own mother. Images of Pecola from Toni Morrison's *The Bluest Eye* float into my consciousness. Pecola's isolation is chronicled as her tale unfolds by those who not only failed to protect her from the odium of the outside world but also participated in its perpetuation. As a result, Pecola becomes the "little-girl-gone-to-woman" (Morrison, 1970, p. 31).

In *The Bluest Eye* (Morrison, 1970), the characters live in constant fear of being cast "outdoors." The "outdoors" is a metaphor for the isolation and vulnerability experienced by impoverished people in everyday life. Furthermore, outdoors becomes symbolic of an inability to have basic needs met—such physical needs as food, clothing, and shelter as well as emotional needs revolving around human connection, love, and acceptance.

While Keisha's identity and naming process begin to unfold, my other student's abruptly came to an end, even before it seems to truly begin.

Understanding the reality and determination of their color allows Black women and girls to steep in their culture and unearth their beauty and strength on their own terms. However, do the terms of self-definition for Black women and girls need to be created in spite of the experiences with and the impact of the dominant culture? Or do the terms of self-definition for Black girls and women need to be created because of experiences with the dominant culture (Bacon, 2009; Jones, 1996)?

Do Black girls need to be pulled aside by Black women and warned of the consequences of race and gender in order to survive? Can we keep Black girls safe by sharing the stories of Black women who have disappeared into the wilderness? Should we maybe whisper into the ears of nine-year-old Black girls that if they choose to wander from the beaten path to find their own voices and follow their own dreams that others may not dare to look for them or even recognize that they are gone? Do we need to hold them even closer to us than other girls, to protect their bodies, minds, and spirits from the outside world and potential harm?

Section Three

Looking for Lost Black Girls

I remember when I was a doctoral student, I received an email from a teacher friend that "Roger," my former student, had dragged a high school girl into the woods that morning and raped her. Although her body would remain mostly intact, her spirit had been left to perish. Shortly following the event, our Black Graduate Student Association would bring to our awareness the story of twenty-year-old Megan Williams in West Virginia. In 2007, Megan Williams, who was a young African American woman with a learning disability, was kidnapped, gang raped, tortured, and brutalized by a group of white men and women, which included a mother and son and a mother and daughter. While repeatedly burning her, ripping out her hair, and stabbing her for a period of weeks, they also doused her in racial slurs. Megan Williams recanted her story for a period of time, although the DNA evidence substantiated her accusations, the accused confessed, and at least one attacker maintained that it did happen even after Megan Williams recanted.

Shortly after that, I heard reports of another brutal crime through the listserv involving a Haitian woman in Dunbar Village, a Florida housing project, who was held, tortured, gang raped, and maimed along with her son by a group of adolescent boys. Although her neighbors heard her scream for hours, no one would help her, report the incident, or even give her and her son a ride to the hospital as they staggered, in the dark, blinded by cleaning fluid. Shortly after, two nine-year-old sisters would vanish, yet their disappearance would not be recorded or recognized by the outside world.

I began to wonder, was there an epidemic in which Black women and girls were disappearing, being cast out, or dragged into the wilderness—physically, emotionally, or psychically—and no one seemed to hear their cries? Did anyone realize they were gone? Did anyone know they ever existed?

I still ask myself these questions, a decade later. Does anyone remember their names? Have we already forgotten the many women to follow them? Sandra Bland, who died tragically in a Texas jail in 2015 after being stopped for a traffic violation. Breonna Taylor, murdered by the police who fired over 30 shots into her home in 2020. What will become of these great tragedies, the massive sacrifices, and the work of the Black Lives Matter Movement and #SayHerName that sought to expose these travesties and many more? Who will speak the names of the victims and share their stories? How will we give voice not only to the contemporary but to the ancient/ancestral pain?

Poet, Lucille Clifton writes of the ancestral pain of enslaved women and men in, "at the cemetery, walnut planation, South Carolina 1989."

She writes for each Black woman of bondage who existed in silence and invisibility without hearing her real name. Clifton writes of the enslaved African American men who existed on the South Carolina plantation she visited who had been so degraded and dehumanized that they were listed in the records as inventory.

She further writes of the enslaved African American women who existed on the South Carolina plantation who had been so marginalized and dehumanized that they no longer even existed, not even in the records as inventory.

I remember the ancestors and I remember those who followed them.

I remember the two missing nine-year-old girls without names in the press. I remember Megan Williams, and the Dunbar Village rape victims. I remember Sandra Bland and Breonna Taylor. I remember Lucille Clifton's poem "at the cemetery, walnut grove planation, south carolina, 1989" and each Black woman and girl who has perished physically, spiritually, emotionally, and psychically before them by being made invisible, nameless, and silent.

I remember the names of my students and I remember my own name. "And I will testify" by writing and sharing the writings of my girls and others to continue to remember their names and my purpose.

This is the poet's charge.

The premise of poetry writing often is situated in the acknowledgment and expression of feelings of isolation, anguish, and a desire to return home. The poet acts as observer, even of her own thoughts, and as participant in the process. And as a Black woman poet, turning from the isolation of writing and searching alone to preempt the disappearance of African American girls, I turn toward the creation of a poetry group for Black women. Together, we sojourn though the wilderness, writing into visibility the experiences of Black girls threatened with disappearance and Black women who have not yet made their way back home. Dr. Shanna Smith, a dear friend and member of my adult poetry group, Black Women Writing, reveals this plight in her poem "My Girls."

My Girls

Two more girls gone yesterday
With twin braids anchoring the sides of their cheeks,
Doe eyes gleaming for the camera-
And it's too bad they are blackgirls
Whose picture only circulated for a moment
Before gone, just like the two.

Why would they, at nine years old,
Slip away from the sidewalk
In the city space that knew them
To direct themselves lost
In their enthusiasm
To be away anywhere a local train took them,
Play grown and invent new selves for themselves
Just across the border?

Did they know no one would look-
Not for black girls in the news,
Not even at nine?
Did some mama tell them
We watch for white, and wonder
More for little whitegirls and women?
Or did the latest lyric only suggest
Black booties, brown thighs, and beige breasts
Are all that's looked for if blackgirls are offering them,
Not pre-pubescent bodies clothed correctly for school?

Two girls found today,
Who wondered away from home
While wandering into our preempted imaginations.
We did look for them, those who noticed
On emailed black underground news-networks.

> We looked into our own mirrors
> And recognized them gone...
> (Smith, in Bacon, 2009, p. 26)

Emancipation from voicelessness and isolation comes from breaking the silence, sharing each truth, and being heard. Liberation is the moment that the poet's words are written and uttered in such a way that in that instant another person has the opportunity to "know" what it is like to be her. Poetry of Black womanhood and girlhood is such a place for the collective voices to pierce the ears of those who fail to hear as they demand and cry "for dignity and restitution and salvation" (Lincoln, 2005, p. 101).

The Power of Poetry

Writing reflects the essence of the person and her life. It is a reflection of the soul. And writing in the voices and reverberations of African American experiences and culture allows the poet to pay tribute to something profoundly beautiful, complex, and rich. The poetic voice unfolds multiple narratives and counter-narratives to the perversion and reinterpretation of the experiences, images, and lives of African American women and girls of those who "otherize" them. In telling the narratives and counter-narratives, it, too, becomes as visible as the girls' and women's lives that there is a necessary obligation to tell not only the sorrow and bittersweet pain but the elation experienced from truth. And to tell the truth is as varied and numerous as the layers of her identity and her many names (Bacon, 2009; Bacon, 2017; Walker, 2003; Walker, 2006).

As the process of creating a self-identity unfolds, how will creating counter-narratives, or culturally responsive poetry, steeped in the culture of Black feminism be experienced by African American adolescent girl poets? Will writing counter-narratives and culturally responsive poetry within this framework become a form of resistance?

Is it possible that if African American adolescent girls uncover the power to name and (re)define themselves, they might not grow into Black womanhood and discover themselves gone? I wish to navigate each pitfall and danger to keep each girl safe. I wish like the Black women in Smith's "My Girls" to whisper into each girl's ear not to wonder or wander from the beaten path and become lost while no one is looking or searching.

Yet in spite of these realities and desire to keep our girls safe, I am still called to remind them to leave the path of the known and follow their "north stars." Black feminist poet and activist, Michelle Sewell expresses this dream in her poem "Girlchild," as she affirms the uniqueness of the girlchild whose birth right is to "always find favor." (Sewell, 2006, p. 272).

It is this yearning to be free that the Black mother/woman dares to instill in her girlchild, although it may take her from the beaten path. The Black mother who nourishes her girlchild's dreams recognizes that while "The white fathers told us "I think, therefore I am," the Black mother within each of us—the poet—whispers in our dreams "I feel, therefore I can be free" (Lorde, 2007, p. 38). Freedom is what the Black mother (figuratively and literally) dreams of for her girlchild, even if it is only a place of solitude in her consciousness (Bacon, 2009).

As the Black mother/woman seeks to preserve the girlchild's life and to keep her safe by protecting her body and spirit from vanishing and perishing in the wilderness, the Black mother/woman recognizes that she must not only allow the girlchild to wander, but she must encourage her to do so to fulfill her dreams. For it is not only the girlchild's body that must remain intact, prevented from becoming one of the physically missing, but her spirit and identity must also be protected from becoming nameless, formless, voiceless, and joyless as a result of being subdued by the onslaught of definitions and expectations of others.

To stay free and follow her dreams, Black mothers/women must encourage the girlchild who is on the brink of womanhood to ward off the urge to become numb beneath oppression and domination. In order to define herself and feel the depth and breadth of her emotions and experiences from sorrow to elation, the girlchild on the brink of womanhood must continue to be free to speak her truths. Only the girlchild's feelings will sustain her poetic spirit and essence. Feelings allow her to maintain her dreams and move her to demand action, change, and visibility.

Black women and adolescent girls have been as highly visible as they have been represented, depicted, and defined by others to not be visible in their true form(s) or true name(s). If fear of shining truth on self-definitions is lifted, if raw emotions and identities are exposed, who will Black women and adolescent girls be for themselves and for one another? Black women must protect the girlchild's voice as much as her physical being, in order to ensure her passage from girlhood to womanhood. Therefore, the girlchild, like the Black woman, must have the means to speak her name(s), tell her truth(s), and reveal her identity (ies), not only for her survival but for her own pleasure. Adolescent girls navigating the path to discovering their own north stars speak to the shared truths and paths between Black women and girls in their writing by sharing their struggles and their joys (Bacon, 2009; Bacon, 2017).

I write through this in my poem "Silence."

Silence

I am silent
Words swirl in my head with the rapid conviction of the turning of the earth but I am silent
There is the feeling of a fist stuck in my airway I cannot swallow it down or throw it up
I am silent
Can they hear me? The gurgling noises coming from my throat?
Can they hear me? Words are forming in my mouth yet when I open to release them the voice of another comes out
Those outside of me are declaring my thoughts
I am silent I am shrinking I am invisible from others to see
I am silent
I am silent
Joanne Braxton breathes life into this quiet, desolate space
Black Women, "We have been as invisible to the dominant culture as rain; we have been knowers, but we have not been known"

I speak up
(Bacon, 2009, pp. 96–97)

Section Four

Poetry: The Creation of Selves

Levin (1985) describes the process of identity creation as the phase of an "authentically individuated self," which begins with the "emergence of guardian awareness of Being" (p. 105). The construction of an "authentically individuated self" is constituted by the "existential understanding of our inherence of Being as a whole" (p. 105). This phase encompasses the journey from an unformed or unnamed identity of "everyone-and-anyone" to the discovery of one's "true-self" through "poetizing motility" (pp. 105–106). And while poetic creations and independent pursuits may in some ways differ dramatically, "...everything individual is always engaged in the process of Bildung [culture, cultivation, cultivated]." And "What constitutes the essence of Bildung is clearly not alienation... but rather the return to oneself..." (Safranski, 1998, p. 14).

Identity construction seems to be linked inextricably to culture. The term *culture* comes from the Latin word *cultura* (latin-dictionary.net), which is defined as the ability to "tend, guard, cultivate, and till."

My students, through the formation of their "authentically individuated selves," tend, guard, cultivate, and till their multiple identities individually and collectively as Black/African American, girls/women, urban/suburban, special education/general education poets. Yet, as they seek to define and cultivate their own "beings as a whole," they often are faced with the need to guard the complexities and dimensions of their racial, ethnic, gender, sexual, ability, and age identification. They also must defy the construction of race and gender created by false perceptions, myths, and stereotypes by the dominant culture, peers, and adult society (Bacon, 2009).

My students lead me through the cultivation process by tending and cultivating their cultural identities as experienced within their age group, location, and contemporary society. As they reap and sow their identities while negotiating external images and contemporary society, I tend to the cultural and racial framework by which students' lived experiences unfold against the backdrop of a historical reality of disparity and injustice, alongside an ancestral heritage of scholarship, creativity, and philosophy. Tension and anxiety surface through tilling multiple identities that seem to call for the ebb and flow of guarding or protecting past and present experiences while exposing and creating multiple identities (Hultgren, 1995). Moreover, the process of Bildung beckons each poet to uncover her true self beneath the many names of her external identity.

What is real? Is real the poet without a name or without a form? Is real the identity that she keeps hidden beneath the surface to mask her most intimate feelings? Maybe real is truth? Or maybe real is uncovering the poet's name or discovering that in her true form she has no name or that she embodies several names. Naming is a secret that responds to the hidden identity and uniqueness of the poet. Naming is also a process that invites the poet to confide, confess, and explore her secret identity(ies) by writing and rewriting her inner life and experiences (Bacon, 2009).

Naming allows the exploration of internal identities, experiences, and inner lives while offering the space to explore external identities. Enveloped in the process of naming for African American poets are the elements of defining, resisting, and imagining cultural and racial images in the abstract and the concrete. It is also at this juncture in exploring the process of naming that I begin to experience and observe the distinctions in language and meaning in the writings of/by my students, published poets, philosophers, and me that emerge through defining and naming race and culture. Naming of poets calls for defining Black, in conventional terms, as a race of people of the African Diaspora (African, African American, Caribbean, and Afro-Latinx).

Blackness also is revealed in terms of a collective experience with marginalization or oppression as shared in my previous poem "These Black Kids." Moreover, Blackness poignantly unfolds as a feeling, image, and description of race, color, beauty, empowerment, complexities, and passion. For African American girls and women, poetic culture tenders definitions, identities, and namings. The poetic culture also offers an identity as individuals and as a collective to transcend labels and names. In transcending the conventional, poets may venture into the realm of imagination or the abstract to connect to their inner spirits or inner lives, their ancestors, or even the universe to call forth their names. This speaks to human freedom. Expressing culture and human freedom under these terms for African American adolescent girl poets and Black women is not passive or detached but rather a conscious, engaged and passionate action. African American adolescent girls uncovering the power to name themselves through writing poetry express their naming and power through "living language," "living words," and. Indeed, a language of the soul.

Becoming

Novelist Opal Palmer Adisa (2006) speaks of the ways in which each character in her writing becomes imprinted in her consciousness and her heart. Her connection to the characters becomes so meaningful that when she writes about the death of a character's father, Adisa weeps for her. Although she is the author, it is almost as if the characters have created themselves and, by that power and virtue, have created her by bringing forth life in the way that lived experience brings forth meaning to the soul and breath to the body (Adisa, 2006; Bacon, 2009; van Manen, 1997). But my poetry participants and students are not characters in a book; they are my students, some of whom I have worked with for years. And I wonder how I will "narrate" their stories without internalizing their pain. How might I become absorbed in this plight, steeped in the issues of justice and Black feminist thought, but not let them become my every thought?

How do I express my "just ire" (righteous indignation) as Freire (2000) suggests, but not become consumed by it, so deeply hurt and exposed by the rage at these injustices? How do I heal my own raw places to separate my experiences from those of my participants and contemporary survivors so the reader can hear the true voices of each participant, and I can maintain my own voice? Every time I sit to write or read their stories it makes me want to weep. Is bringing this forth worth the pain of the creation and delivery?

There is so much to uncover, and I am drawn to the quest of discovering how the experiences of the students will shape the process of phenomenological research. How will my experiences and writing shape the process of phenomenological research? Because I am an educator and a researcher and not a therapist, I recognize that there must be a distinction between the work I have done in formally studying poetry therapy (Hynes & Hynes-Berry, 1994) and my role as an educator, as well as my own lived experience as a poet/writer. Through the process of phenomenology, I believe, questions will be answered or at least explored pertaining to how poetry is experienced by the writers as they uncover the power of naming.

One Day
One day grief will be gone, as even pain does not last, but often is found to be misplaced, forgotten or, if we are lucky, written away. Poems are about sharing the things that we do not want known and saying the things that are "unsayable" (McCarriston, in Moyers, 1995, p. 271). Even in speaking and writing what we do not want known, an undeniable urgency is expressed that can be the difference between a casual utterance and a purposeful declaration. What the poet so often is looking for is the depth and meaning not only of her pain but all pain that frees her yearning for permission to experience deep sorrow in order to simply feel. This is how the poet handles her numbing pain—through consciousness (Bacon, 2009).

Poetry is so powerful a venue that it allows African American adolescent girls the possibility of naming themselves. Poetry is also the venue that enables African American adolescents to be vulnerable, to express a range of emotions in exploration of their many names, forms, and identities unencumbered. But what do African American girl poets who do not have the opportunity to write about their identities, images, and experiences in the mainstream classroom setting do to feel unencumbered and empowered? How do they express and acknowledge their naming? What do African American adolescent girl poets who feel voiceless do?

This is the call to bring forth identities as writers, not just individually but collectively, which also includes a need and responsibility to call forth the names of other girls and women who have been silenced physically, emotionally, intellectually, spiritually, or otherwise. Deep from within there is a sense of knowing that writing poetry individually and collectively is a necessary path to Being.

Section Five

What African American Adolescent Girls Do

The girls' voices, discussions, declarations, writings, and even silences provide the unfolding of answers, as well as more questions, alongside the framework of phenomenology, Black feminism, and intersectionality. It is through phenomenology, Black feminism, and intersectionality that the path of unfolding poetic identities for African American adolescent girls is laid, expressed, and declared for and by the girls and women themselves. Poetic identity is based upon what is experienced, felt, written, and seen within the individual and collective rather than through theories or experiences that have been pre-formulated or imposed.

Moving from behind a pre-formulated or imposed identity theory to poetic identity and naming for African American adolescent girls, Amina Mama (1995) Black feminist, scholar, and researcher, writes of the experiences and places that exist for Black women in *Beyond the Masks: Race, Gender and Subjectivity*. Mama (1995) views identity as subjective, multiple and dynamic, as well as a process in which she herself remains actively engaged as a group member while seeking to empower her research participants.

Much like Collins, Mama experiences identities for Black women as shared, created, recreated, and explored in a variety of spaces from community centers to kitchens. The unfolding of identity and naming occurs through reflections as well as the acknowledgement of participants' and the researcher/facilitator's personal histories. Naming occurs while maintaining an understanding and awareness of individual experiences and uniqueness through lived experiences of Black women expressed in their own terms without being framed around, in contrast to, or defined by the experiences or theories of the dominant culture (in race, gender, or class).

In my study, it is through African American adolescent girls' and Black women's own lived experiences that my poetic naming and identity "theory" is developed and honored. Unlike many traditional and narrowly defined identity theories, Black women's and girls' identities are shaped in and through a historical and social collective consciousness, personal knowledge, discourse, community, poetry, and literature. In particular, "Creative expression of femininity" is illuminated through Black women's poetry (Mama, 1995, p. 148). The path of my phenomenological study is of the voices of the collective and individual through self-discovery, self-awareness, and consciousness that leads to self-inquiry, affirmation, and poetic identities for group members.

It is important to note that as my students get older, it most frequently appears to be the girls in my classes who express reluctance to name themselves, at least in their own terms, rather than using definitions of others. I contemplate how this connects to the intersections of race and gender and the overlapping social injustices steeped upon African American girls and women (Bacon, 2009; Bacon, 2017; Crenshaw, 2016; Love, 2019). Into my consciousness surfaces the quote, "African American girls are expected to get in trouble in ways that damage their own life chances, rather than make trouble for others like the boys do" (Ferguson, 2001, p. 42).

I am challenged by the notion that African American girls are expected to damage their own life chances. If making trouble for others is what boys do, what do girls do? Ferguson's quote is one of the justifications for educators and researchers focusing their attention on boys. However, for me, it is a confirmation of the need to ensure that African American girls are provided a means to share their voices on their own terms to express the pain, fear, and joy they are experiencing even if they are not "making trouble for others" or "damaging their own life chances." And while the educators and researchers in Ferguson's study consider "damaging their own life chances" as limited educational or financial opportunities, silencing the girls' voices, creating isolation, and making them invisible, I assert, damages not only the girls' life chances but the very essence of who they are.

I pause here to additionally highlight the necessary voices of scholars and activists such as Dr. Bettina Love who reveals that Black girls were also subjected to the belief that "they cause trouble for others" (Ferguson, 2001). Love exposes that Black girls were suspended at a rate six times greater than White girls *not* for actual offenses but rather subjective and discriminatory practices, stereotypes, and negative beliefs against Black girls by teachers and administrators based on race and gender. This discrimination is further compounded by skin color in which darker skinned Black girls are suspended at three times the rate of lighter skinned Black girls (Love, 2019).

I Am

How do Black girls manage their pain or express their joy when they are expected to get in trouble in ways that damage their own life chances or are forced to endure stereotypes and exclusion by others?

By writing their feelings and experiences will the girls' essence be uncovered and made visible? African American adolescent girl poets who write their stories, pain, identities, strengths, joys, and successes also write and create their own truths. Declarations and even questions of who they are reveal their inner voices and allow the adolescent girls to uncover their real names and make their identities more visible to themselves and one another. Writing poetry allows adolescent girls to share their lived experiences in such a way as to create and cultivate their essence and inner lives on their own terms without the confines, labels, definitions, or superficial interpretations of others.

Poetry is the means of sharing the things we do not want to say but nonetheless need to speak. Writing reflects the essence of the person and her life. It reflects the soul. Writing in the voices and reverberations of the African American experience and culture allows the poet to pay tribute to something profoundly beautiful, complex, and rich. The poetic voice unfolds multiple narratives and counter-narratives to the perversion and reinterpretation of the experiences, images, and lives of African American women and girls. In telling the narratives and counter-narratives, it becomes as visible as the girls' and women's lives that there is a necessary obligation to tell not only the sorrow and bittersweet pain, but the elation experienced from truth. And to tell the truth is as varied and numerous as the layers of their identity and their many names.

It is the transformation from despair to joy and celebration that Alice Walker writes of in *Anything We Love Can Be Saved: A Writer's Activism* (2012). She describes the struggle of resistance that fosters feelings of being fully alive, turning fear into courage, sorrow into joy, and despair into celebration. Walker reveals the physical and psychic wounding of suffering on the human spirit in her writing on activism. She writes in metaphors, translating her personal suffering and injury into the collective pain and suffering of others who have had their bodies and minds bruised. Like many writers, Walker lends her words to those fearful, reluctant, or too ashamed to speak of their pain.

Unexpectedly, sharing her own words and stories with others to strengthen them and their voices further strengthens her own. As a writer, I also find that the places where I have lent or united my voice with the voices of adolescent girl and women poets has unexpectedly brought me closer to returning to my poetic self.

Walker remembers her journey to this place of devotion to speak out about violence against women and girls beginning when she was thirteen years old. It was the year that she viewed the body of a dead woman whose face had been partially shot off by her husband. A determination to forever remember this faceless, voiceless woman overtook her and demanded that she learn how to tell this woman's story. That demand was finally realized by writing (Walker, 2012). Through poetry and storytelling, we can become a part of everyone whose stories and poems we read. Sharing experiences and stories connects communities, countries, and even continents. It is the stories of others that can uncover our remembrances, inspire us to share our own stories, to create, or recreate our voices, and support and nurture one another.

The phenomenon of the lived experiences of African American adolescent girl poets reveals itself to be about truth, individuality, and the collective sorrow, love, and joy that come from a connection to self and others, the voice and visibility of Black and African American girls, and women uncovering the power to name themselves. We are reminded by literary scholar and author Mary Helen Washington that Black women who "forge an identity larger than the one society would force upon them... are aware and conscious, and that very consciousness is potent" (Washington, as cited in Collins, 2000, pp. 113–114).

Returning Home

> We would like only, for once, to get to where we are already.
> (Heidegger, as cited in Casey, 1993, p. 273)

What does it mean for African American adolescent girl poets to return home to themselves? Can you return to a place that you do not remember? As we journey back to the same place through the wilderness to find our way home, we recognize that home is no longer the same. As nothing goes unchanged, this includes our memories. Casey (1993) reminds us that homecoming, despite the heart's deep yearning, is often brought about through strenuous effort and the surmounting of daunting obstacles. The path leading back to ourselves through writing poetry is not only about who we are but who we will become (Bacon, 2009).

And while we may grasp hands as we travel and unite our voices, the journey of the writer toward homecoming is often a solitary and sacred experience that requires aloneness to unfold. Isolation is not the state or location of being alone. Isolation is not solitary or singular motions of creating words or transforming feelings on the page. Rather, isolation for the poet is frequently the inability to connect the poetry to an almost universal energy or source. And to connect poetry to a universal source is to acknowledge and connect lived experiences and words to the experiences of members of the world: history, family, friends, community, legacy, cultural consciousness, humanness. The process of releasing pain and connecting with self and others through writing moves the writer from a place of sorrow to a realm of healing and of joy.

Silence and Voice
Poets journey through silence, isolation, and introspection to consciously voice and share, phenomenologically mirroring the philosophic transition of poetic expression in solitude, creation, and sharing of lived experiences. Black feminist writers and poets, along with culturally responsive educators, offer further insight and inspiration as well as illuminate the process of discovery encompassed in struggle and resistance. Ultimately, a path is revealed that leads to the voices and lived experiences of African American adolescent girl and women poets. While the emphasis throughout the previous sections has been on finding a voice that is clearly defined by the girl and women poets, it now ventures into the realm of silence, not as muted sounds and voices but rather a purposeful and reflective solitude that poets often experience through sacred moments, memories, and poetic secrets.

This solitude and reflection are the place in the journey of a poet where she introduces and reveals her true self. Eventually revelations from her consciousness are unraveled onto the page. This consciousness often is laced with reflections and memories that hold a "secret privacy" that the poet cannot express any other way but through writing, for fear of losing the richness and depth of meaning by verbal expression, or "deafness" of the listener (Bacon, 2009).

The word *secret*, derived from the Latin word *secretus*, is defined as "separated, set apart, hidden" (van Manen, 1996, p. 12). There are moments and experiences for the writer that are more profoundly felt in silence and secret. These moments are not spoken because there simply is no need to utter them, as feelings that are verbalized are not always adequate for true poetic expression (van Manen, 2005). Silence offers the possibility of communicative secrecy as various thoughts, feelings, or experiences are held inside; it also offers the possibility of existential secrets in which the whole person, not just a thought, of the poet remains a mystery.

How is human existence revealed or concealed through poetry? Is there a "mineness" that is so personal it exacts individual knowing and lived experience, or is human existence revealed through poetry as a general knowing? Is the writing of poetry an individual possession of the poet? How can others hear what is spoken if it remains an entity of individual possession?

Encountering Poetic Silence

The discoveries and encounters of revelation and human existence do not remain static, forced, or neutral through theoretical contemplation. Phenomenology, like the process of writing poetry, does not allow the encountered to be removed, neutral, or dispassionate. The encountered must challenge herself instead to be present, involved and connected to the inquiry. How does the poet experience connection to the inquiry? Will what the poet encounters be heard and felt more authentically in silence?

"There's a big difference between keeping silent and being silent" (Bozzelli, n.d.).[2] Being silent requires that we remain in solitude and yet attuned to the voices and sounds that surround us. It is in silence that we recognize the distinctive chirping of birds, the buzzing of insects in the otherwise stillness of the night. In silence we hear our own true voices resound within us with a clarity and "uncoveredness" we might fail to recognize during our verbal chatter. Silence allows the space for Being in its "uncoveredness" and truth (Krell, 1993, p. 113). It is also in silence that we hear with the sensitivity of the listening ear that connects not only to the words of the poets but to their essential feelings that are not expressed in words (Bacon, 2009; Moran, 2000).

Van Manen reminds us that human scientists need to be mindful of the essential nature of silence, which text and meaning are built within and against. There is a process of uncovering that encompasses experiencing silence, speech, and being silent, all of which rest in the

---

[2] Source unknown. Retreived from a silent retreat.

arms of the poet whose poetry offers truth and meaning that are beyond words. While the process may encompass literal silence, the absence of words or speech, there is also a need for epistemological silence, Epistemological silence is that deep sense of knowing that is often unspeakable (van Manen, 2003).

It is also the feeling or sense that we know more than we can utter aloud. Yet, what we know and cannot speak may be shared by the voice of another—such as the poet. Epistemological silence allows the poet to say what others do not always have the words to express. Van Manen (2003) further expands the meaning of silence for the poet and phenomenologist through ontological silence. Ontology, according to Heidegger, is "the phenomenology of being" (Heidegger, as cited in van Manen, 1997, p. 183). Ontological silence provides the poet with a "fulfilling silence" as it resides in the presence of truth (p. 114). This is a silence of Being and of Life that encourages the poet to return home to her true self.

It is further in the realm of silence and introspection that lived experience is manifested as a unit of consciousness that allows for life to become realized in experience and for the practice of phenomenological research to be as life or to be life. Introspection, reflection, silence, and revelation of self-created transformation are offered as the phenomenology of spirit in which "something is undergone and through it one changes" (Risser, 1997, p. 85). This path or journey to truth requires the exploration of what is hidden, as disclosure of truth leads to consciousness and a higher level of insight. Forgetting the path to truth becomes an absence of presence or an omission of truth that is necessary for the poet to bring forth her voice (Risser, 1997).

For the poet to tell her truths, she must delve into the memory of lived experience and consciousness. The gathering of concerns of the heart gives way to an experience of the collective in which voices and experiences are united to lend shared passion, sorrow, or joy to areas in which there was once despair, absence of presence, or isolation. It is through the voice of collective despair, recognized in resistance and struggle, that a pathway is cleared through the wilderness to strength and insight. Gathering in the name of a collective and individual voice with purpose, intention, and presence evokes remembrances that are unrelenting (Bacon, 2009).

In silence, we listen to our own hearts, needs, the memories and knowledge of our bodies, and the voices, hearts, memories, and knowledge of others. Through philosophy, identity is connected poetically with the body and the memories of the individual. How, then, does identity (as poetic naming) change with consciousness? If the poet deepens her level of experiences (memories or body) to acknowledge the meaning of those experiences, will she uncover her truth and her many names? Does the identity of the poet change as she explores memories and lived experiences, or is she revealing her true identity? What does authentic recognition mean for African American adolescent girl poets cloaked in the names and perceived identities of others and in the epistemic injustice of dominant white culture that discounts their knowledge and experiences?

Truth is derived from the experience of active listening. Within social spheres that uphold seeking and telling truth, voices can be heard and words spoken without fear or shame. The practice of listening for truth offers a space that balances between everything and nothingness in a dance of "harmony and discord, resonance and emptiness, voices and silence" (Levin, 1989, p. 136). The practice of listening to truth (internal and external) and speaking truth cannot be separated, as both require a sense of presence and responsibility.

The journey through silence and listening to internal voices calls for poets and philosophers alike first to travel through the wilderness of an inauthentic or unformed being toward an authentic self. It is in this silence in the wilderness that we may also hear the call for responsibility or conscience. In addition to silence, it is the pursuit of truth wrapped in speech that cannot be false, which is a form of fulfillment that bears witness or testifies not only to personal truths but the truths and revelations of others.

It is through phenomenology and Black feminism that the path of unfolding poetic identities for African American adolescent girls is laid, expressed, and declared. Moreover, poetic identity is based upon what is experienced, felt, written, and seen within the individual and collective rather than through theories or experiences that have been pre-formulated or imposed. As I return to the voices of African American adolescent girl poets, human freedom is a charge of and for collective voices, responsibility, accountability, and naming. Human freedom under these terms for African American adolescent girl poets and Black women is not passive or detached, but rather a conscious, engaged and passionate action. African American adolescent girls uncovering the power to name themselves through writing poetry express their naming and power through "living language," "living words," and indeed a language of the soul.

Finding Each of You

> You must speak the dreams your ancestors only dared whisper.
> (Adisa, 2006, p. 93)

As I call upon ancient foremothers, I invite the writings of Alice Walker (2003) upon this journey. Walker travels to the core of ancestral African American women artists'/writers' despair as she describes how the deprivation of expression and voice drive the would-be writer/poet to lunacy. Walker writes about the Black woman writer of yesteryear who is forced into a place of profound isolation and turmoil as her life belongs to that of another under the oppression of slavery, sharecropping, or cheap and exploitative labor. Yet, the Black woman writer who is finally physically freed from her manacles is still not permitted a gentler fate. The Black woman writer such as Zora Neale Hurston, Phillis Wheatley and others that Alice Walker calls forth may have perished with their names imprinted in the consciousness of many (unlike the enslaved in Lucille Clifton's [2000] poetic testimony) yet still vanished—vulnerable, desolate, and abandoned.

Is this the necessary fate of the Black woman writer/poet whether her artistic spirit is suppressed or expressed? Has she little option but to make the descent into lunacy, despair, or isolation or to travel toward visibility and creative expression only to meet with voicelessness at the end of her journey? Walker writes, *In Search of Our Mother's Garden* (2003), of a grief that Black women in bondage shared. She speaks of the women whose deep creative genius would have been manifested in poetry or art but instead was forced into poverty, oppression, self-neglect, and a life of self-deprivation. Their visions and dreams were never allowed to breathe life back into broken spirits and burdened bodies. And while their bodies may have been shackled, inhibiting them from wandering from the plantation fields into the thick humid air to whisper poems aloud to the southern stars, the poems lived within them. And their legacies are not lost as contemporary African American adolescent girl poets speak the dreams of the Black women before them in their own voices through their lives and creative expression (Bacon, 2009).

Paths taken toward power, naming, voice, and visibility may require risking such ills to journey from self-denial and isolation to writing a way out of the wilderness by way of solitude and aloneness to voice, visibility, and community. And with this, I am reminded of our plight to create our cultural poetic selves through the words of Walker: "I have fought and kicked and fasted and prayed and cursed and cried myself to the point of existing. It has been like being born again, literally" (Walker, 2003, p. 125). Resistance, struggle, and longing are the catalysts for exploration. Walker recognizes that she must leave the comfort of the known works of the teachings of European male poets and forefathers to follow the ancient African foremothers to "where my duty as a black poet, writer, and teacher would take me…" (Walker, 2003, p. 132). And where it takes the African American adolescent girl poet, and the Black woman writer is home.

Some of this journey must be done in solitude, listening to the voice of the poet's inner thoughts, spirit, and memories. Some must be done in active silence while observing surroundings and listening to the hearts, words, and voices of others. And some must be done with an individual voice, speaking her truths for herself, and lending her voice to the stories and lived experiences of others. Yet some of this journey must be done together, joining voice to voice, life to life, and heart to heart in collective resistance, rage, freedom, and uproarious, boisterous laughter. Lorde (2007) reminds us of the journey of the poet's return to herself and her purpose in her poem, "For Each of You." Lorde powerfully asserts that we must be who we are and cherish our Black angels who remain boisterous and drive us to be free).

Audre Lorde, an African American, feminist, lesbian, activist poet/writer, speaks of the process, power and necessity of poetry and voice in her book *Sister Outsider* (2007). In *Sister Outsider,* Lorde names a feminine force and resource that is as powerful, yet spiritual, as the creative expression of poetry writing. Furthermore, she names the feminine force or power erotic—rewriting and defining the term as an expression of a woman's feminine identity, being, and creativity in a form that is not only untainted but embraces pleasure and joy. Erotic energy, according to Lorde, is a form of body knowledge and awareness experienced as feelings or emotions that are not relegated or regulated by a mind that seeks to judge or analyze thoughts or ideas but rather seeks to experience them.

Furthermore, erotic power is not bred in the psyche of societal marginalization or a sense of male domination that seeks to harness a woman's natural power or joy. Rather, erotic power is a feminine energy that embraces and affirms life, and even provides life through its exuberance expressed as creativity, love, and elation. Lorde's naming of the erotic is as expressive and connected as poetry writing, as it offers a bridge from sensual to spiritual, physical to psychic and emotional, and superficial to meaningful.

What are the lived experiences of African American adolescent girl poets writing from their hearts rather than their analytical minds? How do adolescent girl poets embrace their feminine power rather than escape their power and feelings to conform to the expectations and paths of others? Is writing poetry to uncover the power to name who the girls/women really were/are an expression and affirmation of not just the poets' lives but life itself?

Erotic power bridges the connection from grief to joy by creating a pathway through fear (fear of self-definition, empowerment, creative expression, self-knowledge, isolation, feelings/emotions/sensations, body awareness) to the realization and recognition of individual and collective joy and expression. Erotic power acknowledges that suppressing our true expression, stories, experiences, knowledge, or even desires only flame our fears by giving our fears power over us, along with empowering others who might seek to keep us voiceless and invisible. Giving our power over to our fears and to others cripples our spirits and paralyzes our emotional strength and resilience. Feminine/erotic power is the uncovering of muted voices to speak our poetic stories with truth, courage, and conviction. It is also the point where the girlchild on the brink of womanhood wonders and wanders through the wilderness to find her true self without fear or apology. And it is the point where she dares as a poet and as a woman to be free (Bacon, 2009).

Wondering and wandering takes the poet through the "beginning-place" and "end-place" by visiting the "in-between" spaces that eventually lead us home (Casey, 1993, p. 275). According to Casey, homecoming does not require a long stay in the same location but rather a return to that same place. Consequently, the return to that place urges us to recognize distinctive differences or changes that ask us to revisit our memories and past selves (in comparison to who we are now). Homecoming also invites us to reconnect with those who still reside where we once were and who once had meaning in our lives. Homecoming also allows us to yearn for those who have departed from that place (through death, abandonment, or homesteading).

However, according to Casey (1993), homesteading is the journey to a new place that is to become our future home(s). It is that place that is unknown to us even though it might be known to others who have made the journey before us. Homesteading invites us to settle in for an extended period of time. And while homesteading offers the opportunity for us to put down physical roots, it does not need to be literal. Rather, what is essential to the homesteading process is our commitment to remain in a new place/space long enough to build a significant life in that space (Casey, 1993). To ultimately end at the beginning, African American poets and Black women writers must journey through the in-between stages of wondering, wandering and truth saying through a previously traveled ancestral land to return home to themselves and one another.

Moving Between Worlds in the Wilderness: Homecoming and Homesteading

The paths, thoughts, and meanings of phenomenology and poetry dance through, between, and alongside one another. Yet as I deepened my methodological awareness and grounding in Black feminism and culturally responsive pedagogy and poetry, like Alice Walker, I was called to rechart my direction in the wilderness to follow the paths of my ancient foremothers in order to return home and to create a clearing for the new voices of African American adolescent girl poets, Black women, and myself. Culturally responsive poetry, philosophy, and phenomenology are magically and tightly woven to one another through feeling, thought, and practice (Bacon, 2009). As I return to the wilderness, I attempt to conjoin the branches of the poetic, philosophic, and phenomenological not only as practices but as collective voices. Even though they dwell in the wilderness beside one another as trees with "neighboring trunks" as long as they are unknown to one another, they will remain isolated (Hoderlin, as cited in Heidegger, 1971, p. 13).

Reflecting on essential themes such as naming—including what the poets are named by others such as "These Black Kids" (Bacon, 2009, 2011b) and what the poets name themselves—unfolds many layers that offer a pathway for African American adolescent girl poets to journey home. For Casey (1993), homecoming is the return to the same place. It is for the poets a place of their authentic selves, a place of being in their truths, born of remembering and uttering what often is unspeakable. Moreover, this poetic space of homecoming is also offered as a place of homesteading for poets, as it provides the possibility of a new or future home. This place of homesteading invites the girl poets to uncover the power to name and write who they really are, share their voices, or offer new voices to the listening ear. This is also a place that allows for naming to be fluid as the journey of discovery is one of being, feeling, and identity(ies). And it is a place of memories placed beside the creation of whom and what you are now.

African Ancestral Truth Sayers

> Woman's place of power within each of us is neither white nor surface; it is dark, it is ancient, and it is deep. (Lorde, 2007, p. 37)

As I journey into the wilderness to that place of power that is dark, ancient, and deep, I welcome the presence of ancient African poets, truth sayers, and story tellers. For this part of the journey home, I turn to griottes (female truth sayers/story tellers) and griots (male truth sayers/story tellers). I invite ancestral griottes and griots, along with Alice Walker (2003) and Black feminist poets and writers, as I make my way toward culturally responsive poetry through those who continue to cultivate the history and legacy that African American adolescent girl poets and I stand on and build upon.

Griottes and griots enter to till, guard, and cultivate the pathway of knowing and being from the past to the present. They, like the adolescent poets, wear many names from "Jegna" in Ethiopia to "Jeli" in West Africa (Hilliard, 2002, p. 18). Griottes, Griots, Jegna, Jeli are the poets, story tellers, historians, and maintainers of oral traditions. They offer their voices through political commentaries with a sense of knowing that inspires awe. Griottes and griots, in their many names and identities, are avowers of the protection of life, community, and culture. But above all else, they are truth sayers. As in the mythical descriptions of poets who interpret the words of the gods, griots are said to be highly spiritual with so deep an awareness and connection to the higher spirit that they are believed to be as close to God as one can get/be.

I invite and welcome ancestral griottes and griots into this space, in the tradition and legacy of passion, resilience, courage, and resistance as they are known to be extraordinarily fearless. And in this journey through the wilderness of truths, stories, and remembrances, each poet, as she reveals her power to name and calls forth her many identities, invites fearlessness in the face of vulnerability. Like the African American adolescent girl poets and writers, griottes are known to gain their knowledge, teachings and experiences through other women, especially their mothers, sisters, and mother figures (Bacon, 2009; Hale, 1998).

Culturally Responsive Pedagogy

As I continue my journey through the wilderness, I rest a moment to experience the lives and teachings of the philosophers, phenomenologists, poets, and story tellers thus far. I venture toward the path leading to my own poetry group with knowledge of the capacity for wholeness, integration of the senses, and lived experiences, which allow each poet to command fullness of creative expression. Knowledge of the capacity for wholeness is an affirmation of the poet's life, not as an escape from her awareness or an indulgent luxurious expression but as a basic necessity for women and girls.

Yet, before I make my way to the clearing of culturally responsive poetry, I walk through the trees in the wilderness to culturally responsive pedagogy. I begin this part of the journey with Jacqueline Jordan Irvine. I picture her steady and firm hand pressed against my back, guiding me into the realm of methodological practices alongside Gloria Ladson-Billings, Michelle Russell, and bell hooks. This clearing ends with the culturally responsive teaching practice of embracing joy.

Irvine begins her writings with the same captivating "voice" that she sounded during her talk at the University of Maryland that I attended in 2006. Her work reveals the real stories and lived experiences of students in the midst of policies, theories, and statistics. *Educating Teachers for Diversity: Seeing with a Cultural Eye* (2003) begins with the story of Darius, a nine-year-old African American boy living in an impoverished neighborhood. When asked about his dreams and visions for the future, Darius responded, "Lady, I don't see nothing and I don't have no dreams" (p. 2).

Darius's story does not end there for culturally responsive educators as Irvine charge us to act on behalf of children who do not have dreams. Irvine further charges us to recognize that students who do not feel like they have futures in fact do have futures that are "inextricably linked" to our futures as educators (p. 14). This is the charge issued by culturally responsive pedagogy and phenomenology. Irvine further urges us to recognize that we as a society cannot achieve our vision by ignoring children who seem to have none (futures, dreams, or visions) or by naming them as the "other."

I am reminded of the voice of Keisha and other students in my poetry group: those who due to life circumstances did not seem to have any dreams or hopes for the future, while Keisha had many dreams and expressed them with zeal and conviction. How do we help create dreams for those who do not have any and maintain the dreams of those who do? Can we hear both voices and recognize both needs? Can they hear their own voices and the voices of one another and link their own futures and visions? Whether the students have no dreams or dreams in abundance, live in urban communities or attend schools in the suburbs, will writing and reading poetry create a way for them to be heard?

Irvine upholds the call of scholar and culturally responsive educator Gloria Ladson-Billings (1994), for educators to be "Dreamkeepers." Irvine's culturally responsive practices include caring, other mothering, believing in children and their dreams, demanding and expecting the best, recognizing teaching as a calling, and providing appropriate boundaries and structure (Irvine, 2003). Ladson-Billings and Michelle Russell further expand upon these practices by recognizing the essential nature of connecting learning to meaningful lived experiences and making education a part of the students' culture rather than inserting culture into education (Bacon, 2022; Ladson-Billings, 1995; Russell, as cited in Hull, Scott, & Smith, 1982).

Culturally Responsive Uncoveredness
Michelle Russell, author of *Black-Eyed Blues Connections: Teaching Black Women* (1982), connects daily living with history and social justice, resistance, and activism. However, Russell's lessons are uniquely based on the lived experiences of African American women from urban areas. Much like the spaces shared by Black women who exist "beyond the mask" (Collins, 2000), Russell's classroom is constructed in such a way as to create a place where African American women feel empowered to express their voices and the voices of the collective. Her classroom serves as a vessel for "uncoveredness," self-discovery, and remembrances. Through meaningful experiences, a collective knowing and a collective memory are induced, and truths shared. Russell uses the classroom as a safe space, created and nourished by Black women for the purpose of resurrecting change in response to circumstances.

How do African American girl poets use this space? Has this space nurtured a spirit of resistance or created a place of unbridled, uproarious laughter? Is there an individual or collective sense of knowing that the girls uncovered? What stories and remembrances do they share through their poetry?

Into this space now enters joy through Gholdy Muhammad's *Unearthing Joy: A Guide to Culturally and Historically Responsive Teaching and Learning* (2023). Muhammad invites Black genius and liberation as an expression of joy and "shimmer" (p. 34). Joy is further unearthed as not solely fun and celebratory but as the embodiment of learning, self-love, and care for humanity. Through this expression of culturally responsive teaching, joy ignites happiness, truth, beauty, fulfillment, and resolution.

The culturally responsive educator from Irvine to Ladson-Billings to Muhammad, similar to the phenomenologist and the poet, walks through the wilderness of feelings, concerns, joys, and struggles, led and guided by, alongside, and sometimes before her participants to a clearing. She also encourages each participant to be a storyteller, individually and collectively, as a means of transferring knowledge, building a collective memory, speaking truths, connecting to one another, history, and the global community. Each woman, in essence, begins to create her own identity poetically as a griotte/truth sayer (Bacon, 2009, 2017).

The culturally responsive educator acknowledges a social justice, or resistance consciousness. She acknowledges daily living experiences, each participant's life, survival mechanisms, creative expression, and the impact of race, gender, class, sexual orientation, and dis/ability on individual and collective lived experiences. By honoring each woman's life and voice, the culturally responsive educator recognizes there is no aspect of a participant's life or naming that is too trivial to be heard. What is more, the educator acknowledges that seemingly individual lived experiences are often universal experiences (Russell, 1982).

Teaching as Learning
Ladson-Billings (1994) writes of her experiences with successful teachers of African American children. An open flow of ideas and exchanges between the teachers and students was created that allowed the relationship to be fluid, equitable, and connected. The writings of the culturally responsive teacher frequently mirrored practices and thoughts of the Black feminist teacher and the Black woman poet. Black women poets connected to feminine and spiritual energy and power as educators and mother figures, stand guard and till the dreams of African American adolescent girl poets. Black feminist activist, scholar, educator, and writer, bell hooks (1994) speaks of the role of Black women as both teachers and writers.

hooks recalls the tradition within education in which Black teachers connected pedagogical practice to the antiracist struggle. hooks views teaching as a means of resurrecting justice and revolution, and rather than escaping from her role and responsibility as an activist or change agent, she boldly steps into it and claims it. The Black feminist teacher is attached to the outcome of human freedom and builds into the fabric of teaching/education a commitment to counter-hegemony. For hooks, teaching is a service and a means of giving back to one's community.

Yet, while teaching is often seen as a political and professional duty, the practice of writing poetry offers personal freedom and the fulfillment of a serious yearning. hooks uncovers the tension of Black women poets who are connected to revolution and justice as teachers while struggling to fulfill a personal yearning as poets. Their plight encompasses the struggle and commitment to maintain and protect the dreams of the girlchild as well as their own.

hooks (1994) reveals that to achieve fulfillment, a necessary component of pedagogy, involves pleasure in conjunction with resistance and freedom. Excitement, serious intellectual stimulation, and academic engagement are brought about by the development and cultivation of community. Through a genuine interest in one another, the ability to listen to one another's voices and the recognition of one another's presence, community is fostered in and out of the classroom. If we want to assist our children/students in fulfilling their dreams and finding their way to their north stars, it becomes apparent that we must support, inspire, and encourage them. Yet, self-struggle ensues as I explore my role and "requirements" as a researcher, poet, and teacher. How much do I say? When do I lead and when do I follow? Do I release attachment or cultivate it to let my students learn and find their own voices and human freedom? As I reflect on the process of teaching and learning, I return to a place of poetic and phenomenological questioning.

> Teaching is even more difficult than learning... because what teaching calls for is this: to let learn. (Heidegger, as cited in Hultgren, 1995, p. 371)

My study requires that I engage, closely observe, and actively participate in the phenomenological process while "letting" my students learn in their own way, their own time, and through their own experiences. Moreover, this process requires that I "let" my students teach one another and teach me. Hultgren (1995) suggests that the process of "self-struggle" is a necessary component of growth as both a human science researcher and a teacher. As I enter poetic exchange with my students whereby we explore the cultural past and present through poetry and the eyes of adolescents, I allow new ways of seeing to occur. And as the process of self-struggle through teaching and learning continues to unfold, I am reminded of Khalil Gibran's (1966) poem "On Children" from *The Prophet*. Just as he acknowledges that you do not give children your thoughts as they have their own thoughts, I acknowledge that the responsibility of the teacher, at some point, is to learn more than teach.

I draw upon poems, prose, previously written reflections, individual and group discussions, my journal entries, and phenomenology class research papers that the students participated in to recapture lived experiences poetically. Knowing the voices of the former participants of my poetry group and English classes and listening with an active ear to the poetic voices of adolescent participants in other studies and poetry books, I come to this manuscript as a rhapsode, poet, researcher, and educator.

With endings and beginnings, Keisha returns as a guest poet for her homecoming in this new poetic space, having bridged from an African American Adolescent poet to a Black woman writer. Briefly, she offers her voice and experiences as a griotte and poet to and for my present poetry group, who follow behind her to their own homecoming and homesteading.

Inviting New Poetic Voices on the Path: Method for Engagement
In order to allow the engagement of the study to unfold, formal approval and screening were provided by the Internal Review Board at the University of Maryland to work with "human subjects" prior to beginning the program. I also received consent from the office of the superintendent of schools for the county and Read High School's (pseudonym) principal. Furthermore, each participant selected for the group was required to sign an assent form (for minors), and each parent/guardian was required to sign a consent form in order to participate in the study.

The process of selecting a location involved deciding upon a county and a high school. I chose one with a significant number of African American students. Both the county and the school maintain a status of African American students as the majority. This differs vastly from the location, background, and experiences of my previous poetry group and former teaching experiences. Choosing a school where the majority of students were African American eliminated some concerns that I held about not being able to find enough participants in the school where I was employed. It also eliminated some concerns that I had about possibly excluding other interested students when promoting the poetry group.

And while race allows for a homogenous group of participants, Read High School itself offers a great deal of diversity in ethnicity, background, ability, socio-economic status, and location, but what is more important it offers a diversity of voices and lived experiences. Geographically and economically, students represent a rather large range of areas in the county, with some students receiving transportation to attend the high school, which is located in the suburbs of the county, from urban and working-class neighborhoods.

Within the immediate school community, students reside in single- and two-parent family households and live in condominiums, townhomes, and more affluent single-family homes. Read High School also offers a wide range of classes and electives. Students may be placed (and participate) in advanced placement (AP) classes, honors, on-level, inclusion (general education and special education), and self-contained special education classes. Furthermore, the high school is said to have a strong performing arts program with a high concentration of talented, creative, and actively engaged students.

To invite potential students to participate in my study, a flyer was used to advertise the poetry group and information was included in Read High School's newsletter. Moreover, guidelines, requirements and expectations were outlined in a letter distributed to students and parents. Students were expected to attend poetry sessions twice weekly for an hour and a half each session. They were also expected to meet with me, as the facilitator, for 15–20 minutes bi-weekly for individual discussion during student facilitated groups.

During individual meetings, students discussed their poetry, experiences and feelings surrounding their writing, emerging themes, conversations that occurred in the group, and their experiences working and writing in a poetry group for African American adolescent girls. A safe space for poetic renderings to occur is critical, and each member was asked, as indicated in their written guidelines, to respect the work and voices of other members by offering constructive and supportive feedback, and by not laughing or making fun of other participants' writings, readings or expressed feelings.

A meeting and discussion with recommended and interested girls to determine final participation and commitment to the poetry group ensued following the English and performance art teachers' distribution of flyers, newsletters, guidelines, and the collection of poetry samples. In addition, I made visits to a general education English class and a special education English class to discuss the program. I also had discussions with other English teachers, and announcements of the group were made by the principal.

To allow for each participant's voice to be heard and each poet to be visible on her own terms, I shared in writing and during the interest meeting that the group would not exceed twelve. Furthermore, I shared verbally and in writing that each poet would be given the opportunity to reflect and expand upon her poetry experience, individually and collectively, through reading and writing poetry and writing journal reflections (to include her experiences and feelings during participation in a poetry group for self-identified African American adolescent girls) and engaging in discussions with me and other group members. I, too—as an engaged phenomenology researcher, educator, and Black woman writer/poet—wrote reflections, participated in discussions, workshops and shared poetry in and outside of the group to remain actively engaged in the phenomenon and to enhance my lived experiences and connection to the writing process.

Once the consent of participants and parents/guardians was received, I engaged with eight participants in poetic renderings over the course of approximately five and a half months to uncover the girls' experiences with poetry reading and writing to name who they really are. Our meetings, writings and discussions occurred twice weekly for an hour and a half (although they frequently were extended to two hours, and during the last week we met three times instead of two). The focus was on collective voices and the poetic group experience; however, individual discussions occurred both formally and informally on a rotational schedule or as needed, depending on the writing of the participants. These took place during student-facilitated sessions or before or after meetings, in addition to weekly email correspondence with the group.

The program was originally designed to begin with poetry readings by African American adolescent girl poets—primarily from such books as *Paint Me Like I Am* (Writerscorps, 2003), *City of One* (DeDonato, 2004), *Things I Have to Tell You* (Franco, 2001), and *Growing Up Girl* (Sewell, 2006)—and end with their own poetry writing. The participants readily and eagerly shared their own poetry from the outset, allowing the poetry books to be offered as supplemental material or used for occasional writing prompts or poetry samples/models. Furthermore, opportunities for individual and collective discussions and readings of self-selected poems occurred during each meeting. In addition, three published poets were invited to facilitate poetry workshops, and more important, actively listen to the self-selected poetry readings of the girls.

Participants were given the opportunity to respond orally and in writing to one another's poems as well as generate their own works. We further explored connections between their own works elucidating individual and collective experiences within the group. We looked at and drew from expressions of self-identity and empowerment and naming as "I Was," "I Am," and "I Will Be" through their experiences and voices as African American adolescent poets (Bacon, 2009).

Personal and poetic reflections and responses were written in a journal and a notebook in reference to the poems created and read to uncover the power for participants to name themselves. During the first three weeks, students created their own poems by reflecting on topics and themes that resonated with them from the poetry readings. I facilitated the first six sessions and selected icebreakers, poetry, and discussions around friendship to begin building relationships and community within the group based on collective discussions that transpired during "check-in." Students were then invited to select topics and themes that were of importance to them to facilitate and write about for and with the group. The topics selected included grief, sorrow and loss, love, spirituality and God, confidence, goals, self (esteem), and spring (renewal and growth).

Techniques, topics, and poetic structures were "borrowed" or "imitated" on occasion to provide support or serve as a model; however, the ultimate goal and purpose was to generate poems based upon the thoughts, ideas, lived experiences, and poetic identities and naming(s) of the student. In reference to identity and naming, guiding questions included: *"How do you feel you are defined by others?" "How do you define (or seek to define) yourself?" "What names/characteristics describe you?"* A written reflection was also completed during the first and last session. The reflection was based on students' feelings, beliefs, concerns, and experiences surrounding naming as it pertains to lived experiences, feelings, intrapersonal, interpersonal relationships, culture (race, gender, age), etc.

How Will I Name?

Woven into the fabric of questions, naming(s) and affirmations are the works and voices of adolescents' calls and responses to one another and to the voices of published poets. And as we explored the process of "I Am" and naming(s), students began by delving into the process of naming by literally selecting their names (what they would like to be called) for the study and closed with finding "My Real Name." Throughout the study, answers to questions unfolded while other questions surfaced, such as: What was the meaning of the selected name? How will "I Was" "Who Am I?" "I Am!" and "I Will Be" reveal and conceal identities?

By not only reading but writing poetry, African American adolescent girls and young women have been encouraged and empowered to explore various concepts and experiences in order to interact critically and poetically with ideas that pertain to their own lives and naming. Participants explored relevant topics and cultural, collective, and individual experiences to develop a deeper awareness of self and others with the goal of strengthening or cultivating a voice that may lead to (greater) feelings of empowerment, visibility, and expression. Moreover, by honoring the students' multiple identities and names (in reference to cultural, ethnic, racial, ability, gender, class, religious, age, sexual orientation, etc.), a safe space was created that allowed the adolescent girls the opportunity to explore, challenge, and construct individual and collective experiences that may or may not be consistent with external perceptions of students' identities, experiences, and naming(s). To further augment participants' voices, visibility, and co-authorship, within the second month, students facilitated sessions of the poetry group based on a topic of interest to them.

Honoring the Process and Path of Poetry

There were verbal questions that I was unable to formulate in advance, given the nature of hermeneutic phenomenology. For the process of further questioning and naming to unfold, I was required to patiently wait and actively participate in the path of "uncoveredness." We searched for truth and recovered remembrances through poetic words and verbal expression, written poems, journal entries, and reflections. Select audio-taped discussions and readings also served as a formal tool of retrieval to help extrapolate meaning. Moreover, in recognition of the significance of voice and visibility, each participant wrote a final reflection about her experiences with writing poetry in the group.

In honoring and sharing the poetic voice of the girls and me, an opportunity was provided to read and submit their poetry. I was invited to share my experiences in teaching and creating poetry groups for the empowerment of adolescents and women, as well as read poems on local radio programs.

Through the voices and writings of the girls, a path was revealed from the wilderness to wholeness by and through their naming(s). The girls' lived experiences of writing poetry, not only to name but to share who they really are, offer the possibility of creating and hearing culturally responsive pedagogy and poetry as a voice to and for creativity, humor, healing, expression, discovery, resistance, justice, and visibility. As rhapsodes, poets, and griottes, we embarked on this journey individually and collectively, anticipating what might be revealed through our poetry writing and sharing. The next segment reveals the themes that emerged from our experiences in the poetry group.

The collective poetic journey begins by writing and talking "until there are no more words" (Schutz, 2001, p. 4). We journey through this process of emerging voices as poets, rhapsodes, griottes, and *anam cara* (soul friends) of the poet's heart as we explore the lived experiences of writing poetry to uncover the power for African American adolescent girls to name who they really are.

Thus begins this new writing journey and the formation of the Poetic Eight.

Section Six

Becoming the Poetic Eight

The "Poetic Eight" is what the African American adolescent poets of my study have named themselves. Like students who came through this poetic experience before them, their names are brought into or through the world by their external identities, lived experiences, and cultural collective as African Americans, adolescents, and girls on the brink of womanhood. Their identities outside of the group also encompass the various names of honor students, general education students, or special education students. It further includes identities as majority, self-identified straight or heterosexual, self-identified bisexual, or questioning (exploring or explored) sexual identity.

The official members of the Poetic Eight are daughters of Christian ministers, Muslim parents, non-practitioners, middle class parents, working class parents, and single fathers. They wear size zeros and fours and eights and size sixteen. They wear short hair, medium-length hair, natural hair, straightened hair, twists, and braids. They also wear the names of girlhood as "good girls," "tough girls," "strong girls," "lost girls," "found girls," "accomplished and ambitious girls," "outsiders," "insiders," "struggling," and "scholars." As daughters and girl children, they have been given identities and names of "beloved" adopted daughter, foster care daughter, biological daughter, stepdaughter, big sister, half-sister, granddaughter, surrogate mother, niece, the daughters of mothers living, deceased, never known, by birth or adoption/choice, and daughters of God (the universe).

And while these identities and names may offer some insight into who these girl poets are or what they have experienced, they do not define them or their poetic uncovering. The girls themselves reveal who they are through their writing and their own naming—by, through, in spite of, in support of, and because of their external identities and many names. They unfold who they are in the poetry that follows. Each of the eight joined the group for different and varied reasons. Blue and Mishaps became members of the group to write through the deaths of their mothers and share their stories. They have shared their poetry with others not only to write through their own grief but to help others find their words and voices through their stories and poems. Divine Diva participated not only to write her poetic story (ancestry, family, culture, struggle, loss) but to have it heard and understood(Bacon, 2009).

Family joined the group to write through the loss of her biological family and to overcome her stage fright and stuttering, while Camille joined to find and share more of her voice through her writing. Lenash came because she loved poetry and wanted to share her talent. Queen of Hearts became a member to explore her interest in creative writing to prepare for college, and KiRe, who initially joined for community learning/service hours, developed a deep desire to be a published poet and performer. As each embarked on fulfilling her own individual mission, she found not only what she was looking for but a new level of voice and empowerment that encompassed the collective experience of hearing and supporting the others' missions and poetic journeys. As I reflect on the lived experiences of the members of the Poetic Eight, who were called to enter into this space by and through the name poet, I wonder if their naming unfolded differently than the girls before them because they named themselves poets. Did their naming change as they revealed "I Was" to "I Am" and "I Will Be"?

Building the themes around the students' lived experiences and poetic renderings continued to unfold against the backdrop of phenomenological and Black feminists' voices. However, the return home (homecoming and homesteading) in my study remained the pathway to a clearing in the wilderness. As the next segments of my study unfold, I am led by the voices of my poetry students and my own poetic journey with them to their naming(s). Their poetic voices, writings, and even silences helped guide a way through fragmentation to wholeness. The journey begins with the lived experiences of grief and loss in poems, such as Mishaps' "Suffocation," written about the death of her mother. I connect her writing as a motherless daughter to the grief of Zora Neale Hurston, along with Alice Walker, Toni Morrison, and other writers and poets (Bacon, 2009, 2017).

As I revisit this process of grief and healing, I do so primarily through the journey of Blue and Mishaps. This journey allows for the writing to grow alongside the writers, as well as to bring about powerful closure as Blue reenters this space in 2022/2023. She is no longer an African American adolescent girl but a Black woman in age, lived experience, and consciousness whose reflections close this book.

As I return to the cultivation of the Poetic Eight in which Blue and Mishaps were members, I offer shortened poetic pieces or specific lines in this iteration, drawing on the experiences and reflections of the poetry group rather than full poetic works and pieces.

I now return to "My Girls" through my own experience as a Black woman writing in solitude and in sisterhood.

Haunting Suffocation

In March of 2008, I return to Holy Cross Abbey. It is my third visit, second stay in the retreat house, and first time inviting a guest into such solitude to accompany me along this portion of my journey at the abbey. I travel with dear friend and member of Black Women Writing Shanna, whose voice and poetry ("My Girls") enter through "Looking for Black Girls." She houses a similar identity and spirit to my own as a protector of the stories, visions, and memories of Black women writers. Like me at this time, she is also an African American woman writer/poet, doctoral student, and educator. On this journey, we are both accompanied by our journals, texts, poems, messages, novels, and numerous stories, but most of all we bring with us the haunting spirits of the Black women whom we carry in our own knowing and in our own hearts (Bacon, 2009).

The abbey is sprawling, and in this space we share ideas and feelings that can only reside in the openness and vastness of the acres of land and freshness of air and space that extend as far as you allow your sight to see. Few people or even trees fill up the acres, but the spirits of these Black women whom we bring with us (or maybe who were already here) fill the land. Some of the women are from fables, characters in books; others are leaping from the pages of slave narratives and from the voices of revolutionaries, activists, Black Panthers, teachers, mothers, and poets. They are courageous; they are afraid; they are fearless; they are proud; they are fragile; and they are connected, free, and knowing. They are unyielding, not only with fortitude, but as fortitude. They simply are as they are and want to be in the space of "I Am." And they are us in our many names and forms seeking life and expression through our voices, knowing, and written words. And they are the voices and lived experiences of the African American adolescent girls of my study who named themselves the Poetic Eight.

At nightfall, Toni Morrison (1987) enters the walls of the abbey through *Beloved*. Morrison's book concludes with the collective strength of Black voices that send the haunting spirit back home to rest for good. Through this fictional account, I enter into the "haunting" of our own poetic space by the memories and remembrances of my students, beginning with Mishaps and Blue. I wonder if Mishaps' and Blue's stories, memories, poetry, and strength of collective voices will forever honor the presence of their deceased mothers and loved ones. By writing these Black women home, are they (not only their mothers but the girls themselves) able to find reprieve from the grief and sorrow that suffocate them and return to joy and life?

In the morning, as our footprints rest on the monastery trail, which is sacred and serene, the voices and spirits of those still living as well as departed come alive. And as I make my path, I step into the footprints of Zora Neale Hurston (1942), who left *Dust Tracks on a Road*. I ponder the ways in which Mishaps and Blue might carve out a path in Hurston's footsteps or, instead, follow a trail not yet traveled to a clearing for themselves and other girls who are grieving and searching for their mothers. They write their way to meaning through memory and body, as "mommy hunger" and "suffocation" become markers to find their way home (Bacon, 2009, 2017).

We step cautiously alongside a bubbling body of water next to our trail. The water flows beneath a bridge and spans the length of a cleared wooded area of our path until we turn away from it to return to the abbey. As I look closer into the tranquility of the water, I notice circles forming and churning. The circles move slowly and methodically until they begin to embrace greater force and vigor. There seems to be a beckoning to face the growing turmoil of the water rather than return to the safety of the abbey walls. Beside the bank, my friend and I begin to fade as I, instead, imagine the creations of Toni Morrison's *Sula* (1973) emerging from the water's turmoil. Sula stands beside the river with her best friend Nel watching helplessly for the little neighborhood boy playfully tossed into the mouth of the water, never again to reemerge.

Stepping back into the poetic waters of a journey toward homecoming and homesteading is a trying one at times. I remember the voices, writings, and lived experiences of the Black women who have walked this path before me. And I remember my former students, like Keisha whose teachings, "learnings" and writings spanned nine years before those of the Poetic Eight. I remember the lived experiences of my own poetic journey and reflect on the work of the journey ahead (both the tremendous joys and the sorrows of the unfolding of the individual and the collective lived experience through the wilderness). And I am now drawn to Mishaps' writings, "I hate that the world is round because history repeats itself and so does my hurt..." (Bacon, 2009, p. 134).

Will the girls uncover their power through their writings if history is to repeat itself in their experiences of grief? In what way do they unfold their remembrances and the experiences of Black women writers who have gone before them?

As I remember the names of the real and of the dead alongside stories, fables, and metaphors of creators (such as Morrison), I begin to recognize that I am not helpless in this writing process or fear-stricken like Sula and Nel by the bank, waiting for the drowning boy to reemerge. Rather, I enter into this space as rhapsode and writer/poet alongside the voices, stories, memories, and lived experiences of Mishaps, Blue, and other members of the Poetic Eight. And while their memories (and mine) may suffocate them (and me) at times, they will not drown them (us). Instead, the girls (and I) will keep rising to the top of the water as they right/write and rewrite their lives and their loved ones and experience reemergence, homecoming, and homesteading as poets and griottes (truth sayers). But first, we must make the journey through feelings of suffocation as a motherless daughter led by Mishaps.

Suffocation

> My lungs give out on me...
> This suffocation is excruciating
> My mom is gone now all I have is my dad...
> Its suffocating, but it just wont die
> I believe this suffocation will remain for the rest of my life
> (Mishaps, in Bacon, 2009, pp. 135–136)

Motherless Daughters

Like the poetic spirits that rise through Morrison and Hurston, Mishaps' poem haunts this space. Her grief, confusion, and despair over the recent death of her mother does not line the air with a faint and distant haze but rather engulfs the space in such a way as to consume enough oxygen to leave Mishaps' listeners gasping for air as well. "Suffocation" is not an invitation for discussion and un-concealing, but a directive. "Suffocation" moves us to dig in the soil past delicacy and polite prescriptive conversations to what lies beneath. Uncovering the underbelly of death where piercing grief and loss reside keeps one digging with such tenacity that the hands that reemerge are so raw they can no longer feel. It is through this digging that Mishaps' unconcealing begins. Yet, she sheds no tears as she reads "Suffocation." And as she shares the death of her mother with the members of the poetry group, it is with eyes directed not toward ours but through them. Her gaze does not move or waiver any more than her voice does. And it is with her reading and unearthing that "... death stirred from his platform in his secret place in our yard, and came inside the house" (Hurston, 1942, p. 63).

Zora Neale Hurston in her autobiography, *Dust Tracks on a Road*, unfolds her grief and emptiness following the death of her mother as she breathes these words into the numbing silence, which is echoed in the lived experiences of Mishaps and Blue. "That moment was the end of a phase in my life. I was old before my time with grief of loss, of failure, and of remorse" (Hurston, 1942, p. 64). Braxton further chronicles Hurston's experiences as a motherless daughter in her book *Black Women Writing Autobiography* (1989). She shares Hurston's reflections of being different from other people because of her loss, which she did not want others to uncover. Hurston's pain and isolation created a weight and longing to be like everyone else and to escape her feelings of "cosmic loneliness" (Braxton, p. 149). Nevertheless, death is a visitor that once seeking your presence and attention knows always how and where to find you (Bacon, 2009; Bacon, 2011b).

All Tapped Out

> I'm all tapped out ...I cry no longer cuz I've stored away all my tears...
> (Mishaps, in Bacon, 2009, p. 137)

Mishaps' feelings of suffocation cause her to become emotionally tapped out. She ends her poem "All Tapped Out" by writing, "But in the end when I'm all tapped Out." "Don't worry I don't just hate you... and you." "I hate me too" (Mishaps, in Bacon, 2009, p. 137). Feeling "All Tapped Out" it is only the pain that she describes in "Suffocation" that remains to remind her she is still living. Fear and hatred have become her secret companions; they travel beside her as the presence of death (Bacon, 2009).

O'Donohue (1997) offers death as the presence that surrounds us but remains a secret companion to whose presence we are blind. The expression and presence of death is said to greet us when we are frail, hurting, vulnerable, or negative. My experience of reading and writing grief reveals, however, that death meets us during the times of clarity and bravery when we dare to look closely into her face and feel her pulse connecting to the rhythm of our own lives or another's. Death requires a surrender and acceptance of not only its process and nature but of the process and nature of oneself.

In surrendering and accepting our process and nature, Rilke (2005) charges that it is death that forces us to increase our strengths and brings us more deeply into the rhythm of life. As this process of grief and surrender begins for Mishaps and the other adolescent girls, I wonder what they might create and achieve, not in spite of their pain but because of their "grief of loss, of failure, and of remorse" (Hurston, 1942, p. 64). What is it that their pain needs? More important, what in them needs their pain?

Liberation from marginalization has come from sharing the stories and voices of others that have urgently needed to be told or otherwise not heard and "held up" with the merit and tremendous worth that they deserve. Yet, as I pause to look back on this work and the stories that were born many years ago, I am drawn to new revelations and lived experiences that have broken my heart wide open. Both open to the sorrow of life's transitions along with life's joys and miracles.

I reflect on the writings of author and psychotherapist, John Welwood, who is known for his integration of psychology and spirituality. Welwood (n.d.) writes, "It is only through letting our heart break that we discover something unexpected: the heart cannot actually break, it can only break open."

As I turn to life and death, to beauty and grief, I now turn to my own path in becoming a mother and a motherless "child" in what feels like one suffocating and life-giving breath.

Expecting my first child, a daughter of my own, and the sudden death of my mother before my baby could come into the world, in a span of three to four months death, and life became intertwined as one heartbeat living within and without my body. The death of my mother, whom I still so desperately needed, occurred alongside the fullest expansion of my heart, with the birth of my baby girl.

Having walked this path of the pain of loss and grief (death and abandonment) of my students, participants, friends, poets, and writers, I return to the path of my participants' writings by embracing my own identity and unfolding as a motherless daughter and as a mother. I am reminded through the loss of my mother that what the poet so often is looking for is the depth and meaning not only of her pain but all pain that frees her yearning for permission to experience deep sorrow in order to simply feel (Morrison, 1973).

This is how the poet handles her numbing pain—through consciousness. And with consciousness and purposeful declaration, I, too, am called to share and say the "unsayable" through my writing and poetry with the truth, candor, and courage that I ask for and see continuously displayed by my students (Bacon, 2009).

Motherhood

>It was sudden when my mother left the world
>Spirit's voice awakened me that morning
>A message so clear it startled me with its
>Reverberations in my ear
>Urgently directing me to call her
>This would be the last time we talked
>This would be our final good-bye
>
>When my mother left the world, I did not
>Know how to live without her
>Her death yanked my beating heart from my chest
>
>How does a mother-less daughter now come to
>Motherhood?
>
>My baby girl would be born only a few months later
>I believe their spirits met
>I believe they danced together and around each other
>In absolute completeness
>My heart taken from my body when my mother died
>Now vigorously beats outside my body through my daughter
>
>As once told to me, "Being a mother is living with your heart
>Outside your body."
>(Bacon, 2023)

With this knowing, I return to Mishaps and Blue with A Motherless Daughter's Poetic Bleeding.

A Motherless Daughter's Poetic Bleeding

Mishaps carries a tragic burden, which does not belong to her and is well beyond her years. She carries the feeling, upon finding her deceased mother, that she could have saved her from death's grip. And she carries with her the belief and burden that she had the power to save her mother from a life of domestic violence, pain, and poverty. It is this pain that compelled her in past years to turn to physically bleeding it from her body that she now instead spills with words onto the pages of her poetry. "When I'm writing it helps me to relieve what's there for that moment...writing became my knife [to bleed out the pain], my sword, my protection. I just use it to the best of my ability. I just use it as much as I can" (Mishaps, in Bacon, 2009, p. 139).

Writing for Mishaps and many of the other girls is the return and uncovering of the power they have been robbed of through life circumstances and experiences. Once a motherless daughter begins this journey of discovery and rebirth through writing, there is often no turning back. For daughters whose worlds have been built within that of their mothers, there is no place except within to go home to. With this sorrow and determination, Rilke (2005) beckons the writer to take her "affliction and bliss" (p. 108) of life and relationships into her work.

Writing is the expression of deep pain and profound joy. Yet, in other areas of her life outside of her writing, the poet must refuse to accept being made to suffer. Writing for Mishaps and many of the other girls is a "face-off" with death in order to overcome pain, fear, and other negative experiences in order to return to the living without guilt or remorse. Writing is also their release of sorrow, by choice, of the secrets that would otherwise consume them. It is also the hatred and pain they feel over being left among the living. Mishaps further shares her deep feeling of fear in "To Be Me."

> To be me is to be hated
> Loved and then traded...
> And as the wind slows my tears run...
> Tears for lost ones...
> (Mishaps, in Bacon, 2009, pp.139–140)

Writing is the path for Mishaps to be the voice for her mother and for her own pain. Writing is also the path for Mishaps to recreate herself and her life story. As Mishaps and I talk about how she can "rewrite" her life story, she quickly responds she would write her mother "back to life": "And I would just let my life play out. There are a lot of things that go on that I can't stop. I want to but I can't." Mishaps unravels her story and confusion around her grief and remorse onto the page for others to hear and understand her. She writes through her suffocation and self-destruct[ion], ending her poem "Self Destruct" with "To die is to kill" (Bacon, 2009, p. 140).

"Self Destruct" is written to voice the feelings that surged within her after her mother's death a year ago, causing her to contemplate taking her own life to end her grief and suffering by joining her mother. As she safely unravels her feelings of wanting to end her father's life for the pain he caused her mother to endure by battering her, she comes to understand and share in our discussion, "... killing someone else is both to kill another person and killing yourself. It's not what I would want to do... And I couldn't do something like that. To take another life [mine or someone else's]. I don't want to set myself up because what is done in the dark will be revealed [to God]. So, I can't kill myself [and I can't kill another]. To die is to kill." But as her rage subsides, numbness seeps in. The numbness is buried so deeply in her body she once wanted to dig into it to feel again. She is the Black women in the wilderness "ejecting fear" and "regurgitating hate" (Bacon, 2009, pp. 140–141).

Mishaps' writings, reflections, and discussions around "Self Destruct," "Suffocation" and "To Be Me" resemble the public voice described by Braxton (1989) in diaries written as autobiographical reflections of African American women writers. Rather than maintain a private account, the diaries of the African American women writers in Braxton's book unfold a tradition of writing with a public voice. Their writings reflect a struggle that honors their intelligence, sensibility, knowing, resistance, and truth. Through public voice and uncoveredness, "black and female poetic identity" of "restoration and self-healing" (p. 85) is created and expressed.

Poetic Calls to Death

Death and violence cling to Mishaps and suffocate her spirit. How will she send these haunting spirits home? The story of *Beloved* (Morrison, 1987) requires sending ghosts and demons home. However, for Mishaps, her lived experience requires sending the presence and images of even goddesses, saints, or martyrs home to be free and find her own path.

Until now, Mishaps is alone in this poetic process, but through the group she is offered a sense of knowing in response to her "Suffocation." This sense of "knowing" begins to sooth the gaping wounds, quiets the violent, turbulent, sounds, and gives another voice to what is not spoken. Through my invitation to enter into this space alongside Mishaps, Blue and other members of the Poetic Eight, offer their poetic responses to Mishaps' "Suffocation."

After poetic snaps, nods, and sighs, epistemological silence reenters the space. It is then that I invite the poem to be read again but this time as a collective voice. We begin with the reading of Mishaps and go around the room, each one of us reading only one line from her poem. After the poem is finished, I ask each member of the group to call into the once silent space a line or lines (even if the lines have been called out before) that resonate with her (connect with a memory or a feeling or simply speak to her in any way). As we close the call and response, I offer the opportunity for each girl to write a poem to Mishaps by beginning with one line from "Suffocation," followed by her own words. By using the first line of Mishaps' poem, each girl creates her own poetic voice.

> Breathing became (ten thousand five hundred seventy-two percent) less easy…Being drowned by my feelings…
> (Camille, in Bacon, 2009, p. 142)

> This suffocation is the thing that stops my heart…
> (Lenash, in Bacon, 2009, p. 143).

Mishaps' mouth begins to expand into a smile that takes over her face and casts light from her eyes as she shares her experience of being heard. "It is like someone finally walking in my shoes. It is as if they understand me. It feels good." Mishaps writes in her reflection following the conversation, "It made me feel like if I hurt so do others and they need my help as much as I need others help…"

Camille offers her voice as a griotte and Lenash as a rhapsode; however, it is Blue who enters this space as an *anam cara*/soul friend (O' Donohue, 1997). Blue's role is unfolded in the following sections. As an anam cara, Blue lends her lived experience and her heart to Mishaps' sorrow. The tears Mishaps does not shed as she reads "Suffocation" are shed instead by Blue. It is Blue's sorrow as a mother-less daughter that allows her to offer her pain, compassion, and tears when numbness prevents Mishaps from expressing her own sorrow (Bacon, 2009).

Poetic Numbness and Our Emotional Lives
We often deem "Humanness" as the negative side of ourselves. Our humanness houses frailty, hurt, vulnerability, imperfection, and pain.

However, it is often those traits, that we name negative that become our greatest tool for creativity, renewal, and rebirth (Bacon, 2009). O'Donohue (1997) urges us to welcome home our "negative" qualities, rather than banishing them or repenting for their existence. Acknowledging and feeling our pain bring harmony and unity into our lives. Feeling our pain also allows us to accept our poetic identities and many names. As we explore our humanness, we bring into awareness that "at the deepest level of the human heart there is no simple, singular self. Deep within there is a gallery of different selves" (O' Donohue, 1997, p. 113).

Alice Walker (1983) writes, "I hated myself for crying, so I stopped, comforted by knowing I would not have to cry—or see anyone else cry—again" (p. 246). Walker reminds us that our emotional lives and growth can be stunted by negative experiences and fear. These lived experiences can take us from our loved ones (in body and spirit) and from love itself. Negative experiences that cause numbness can also push us into isolation, gnaw at our truth, and diminish our feelings of self-worth and belonging. Furthermore, fear and sorrow can take us away from life, even before our physical demise as, "All fear is rooted in the fear of death" (O'Donohue, 1997, p. 204).

Turning toward our "different selves" frees us from the fear of death that casts a shadow on our true existence and our lives. Embracing our different selves is to realize who we really are in our many names and poetic identities. Truth and self-awareness cannot exist in the same space as denial and fear. Truth is un-concealment that begins by digging beneath the soil and uncovering the roots of the trees in the wilderness, whose existence evaded us because of our own isolation. Poet M. Eliza Hamilton (1994) writes that to end the journey of fear, one must uproot oneself (and one's emotions) to root oneself again. While the process of uprooting oneself may feel like a death, as it requires letting go of the past, it is actually a rebirth that comes from being renewed.

Poetic Re-Emergence from a Partial Death.
The path for Mishaps and other members as motherless daughters, exposes a deep sense of self-struggle. Yet, the experiences with "different selves" move the Poetic Eight toward intimacy, knowing, and self-acceptance. This is also "a pathway to meeting with a life-long friend from the deepest side of your own nature" which allows one to be fully alive (O'Donohue, 1997, p. 201). However, the need to repent for "imperfections" or "negative" qualities still often drives this journey through both the wilderness and the desert. During those moments of

being driven by the need to repent, the Poetic Eight must use their imaginations, like poet Oliver's (1986) "Wild Geese" to find their way home. Loneliness and isolation are softened by the poetic process of telling despair, and hearing the despair of another, for self-forgiveness, acceptance and belonging. Oliver's poem echoes that one is not required to be forgiven by walking on one's knees.

In the beginning of this journey, Mishaps walks on her knees, repenting for something that she has not done and an act that she cannot undo. The journey is arduous, and as Mishaps begins to tell her despair and hear the despair of the other girls in the group, she writes her way from an emotional death to revelation. Moreover, to arrive at self-acceptance and belonging, Mishaps, along with the Poetic Eight, collectively gaze into the face of despair.

Revelation and uncoveredness are often experienced as a partial death for the writer as it is so personal, passionate, and laborious a process that it can rob the spirit while transforming it. Many who write poetry or autobiographies experience a sense of self-awareness or self-healing through creative transformation, revelation, or change. Writing during this process is sparked by an (inner) crisis, incident, or event. During the event or crisis that brings about a change or acknowledgement in identity, writing can serve as a refuge for the poet.

>How will I live knowing Death is right around the corner..."
>(Mishaps, in Bacon, 2009, p. 147).

With each work writers create from their hearts reflecting their lives, truths, memories, and souls, the "living word" is ignited and restored. Moving from destruction to reemergence requires a rebirth through creativity. Through this restoration and reemergence process, Blue is able to address the presence of death.

>Look to the sky and still don't understand what's going on...
>Like a repeating song
>Singing Momm, Mommy, come and find me
>But I haven't found me dealing with insecurities
>Pain gushes like blood from a wound
>Feeling like a balloon thoughts
>And pain
>I want to go insane still I look to the sky
>Feeling high on this drug of pain
>And still don't understand what's going on in my veins a blood

> boil
> From blood pressure
> Not having my mother is
> Why I wonder why am I here
> Hearing rolling thunder
> Wonder wonder
> But still don't understand
>
> Whats going on
> (Blue, in Bacon, 2009, p. 148)

Blue now enters into a symbolic dialogue with her mother, as well as with the group. Through her reflection, she shares her experiences with her own partial death after the loss of her mother.

> I'm tired just the other day we went past the cemetery. We even drove down the road the same road we took after the funeral. I couldn't breathe. I felt the pain in my heart. My sense of thought froze my body turned cold. Mom I can't even look at your picture any more... I'm tired I'm ready to be with you. I miss you with a passion. Mom sleeping on your pillow is not enough. I'm tired of trying to be looking to be okay with this life decision. I'm bless[ed] with the house I'm in now [living with her father, stepmother, and stepbrother after her mother's death] because if I wasn't in here now I wouldn't be here in school maybe even living. I miss you mom!!
> (Blue, in Bacon, 2009, p. 148)

At one time or another, each poet experiences "desolate solitude." It is often a state that is necessary to spark the transition or call to voice and freedom from silenced emotions. Delving into the emptiness and places that are numb can beckon us to write our emotions. And through the process of writing and weaving between concealing and revealing, individually and collectively, "disguised women... whose identity[ies] remain partly obscure" begin to unfold (Braxton, 1989, p. 24). For Blue, will delving into her emptiness begin to sooth her desolate solitude? How can her dialogues with death and grief allow her to breathe again and begin to heal her heart?

Invisible Poetic Tears

In response to Blue's revelation, each girl enters the dialogue by connecting stories of funerals, wakes, partial deaths, numbness, and emotion. And with the revealing of emotion, anger and pain, tears seem to be missing again. Blue's tears are at the surface of her eyes, but this time she looks away. What does it mean for Blue when she writes of her mother and as the tears well up in her eyes, she forces them back down? Will her poems write her back to the place she remembers, not only in her mother's heart but her own? What happens to motherless daughters once she is gone? "...Mama dies at sundown and changed the world. That is, the world that had been built out of her body and heart" (Hurston, as cited in Braxton, 1989, pp. 147–148).

Mishaps' writings join Hurston's words and Blue's now-silenced emotions, "The perfect mother... if you were here you'd be as perfect now as you were then...I wish I could have been the perfect child. If you were here you'd tell me I was...I was as perfectly unperfect as you..." Blue is the color of poetic emotion laced with tears of fright, sadness, loss, frustration, disappointment, and loneliness. Shared by many members of the Poetic Eight are feelings of loss for mothers who have died or were taken by other means (including foster care or abandonment). As Blue, Mishaps, Family, and Divine Diva grieve for their losses, they do so by shedding invisible tears.

Family, who has named herself for the family that she lost, now enters this space as a motherless daughter. She was permanently taken from her parents to be placed alongside her siblings in foster care. During the poetic process, she grapples with her grief and feelings of abandonment.

Camille enters this space alongside Family. Camille has renamed herself her birth name (which was changed after her adoption). She was adopted by a loving family and has seemingly erased her memories as a motherless daughter. What does or will this connection to grief through and by the other girls mean for her?

In the presence of Camille's and Family's silence, Divine Diva shares her grief. Divine Diva has named herself a Divine Diva to the world, yet a burden to her parents. She writes through her sorrow as a motherless daughter, having spent her young years being shuttled between her parents, grandmother, uncle, and other relatives.

As the adolescent girls reveal their pain and suffocation, Nietzsche's (2006) reflections serve as a reminder that the problem for women is that they are rarely allowed to be authentic in the expression of their pain. Rather, women live out their lives as if actors on a stage. Often, women sacrifice who they really are to play an object or role for others (for parents, children, lover/partner) and their needs, wants and desires. Learning to play an inauthentic self, rather than their true selves, is often the process of transitioning from girlhood to womanhood (Babich, 2006).

However, the girls in my poetry group express the voice of a new generation of women as African American adolescent girls on the brink of womanhood. Their lived experiences and stories are shared from behind the mask and rarely conform to hegemonic images and ideas of womanhood. Throughout their declaration and affirmations of strength, independence, resilience, and even pain and fear, there is a refusal to see themselves or be seen by others through the lens of victimization. The adolescent girls in my study seem to live almost virtually, free of multiple oppressions and silence except when they cry. How has the expectation of strength and independence of African American adolescents, on the brink of Black womanhood created its own stage of silence and deafness?

Strong Black Women Don't Cry

I haven't cried like I needed to
I don't know what to cry about
I tend to get sad but nothing ever happens
Mainly people may have noticed that when
I cry there is something really wrong with me.
I never cry over little things
Or someone trying to hurt my feelings.
But I know one day it will all come out.
You will see what my life is really about.
(Blue, in Bacon, 2009, pp. 152–153)

The girls in my poetry group, in spite of their awareness of disparity, express a tremendous and outspoken confidence, sense of self-worth, and freedom. What is more, they seem to have maintained a sense of wonder and wander of the "girlchild" in spite of their transition into womanhood. Yet, when grief strikes them, why are they, as strong Black women, often reluctant or afraid to cry in front of one another?

And while marginalization cuts across color, ethnicity, and socioeconomic status, Black women and girls, especially from urban areas, have been stigmatized based on race and gender and, thereby, forced to endure societal hostility, stereotypes, distortions, and victim blaming. Societal marginalization and hegemony have created images that have controlled, constrained, and suffocated choices and options for survival. Societal marginalization has also created a climate of silence by those who must share their stories and deafness by those who must hear them (Richie, 1996). Blue unfolds her feelings as a strong Black woman who does not cry in her poem "You Missed Out."

You Missed Out

You missed out on my cries
You left confusion inside
Being a problem child

Hiding from the lies
I didn't care if you wasn't there
All I need was my mother

That's why I never stop to wonder
Where you was or
What a life without you would
have been
But now I see what could have been
Now I am wishing
For that life again
But all I have is …
Hurt and lies from U
To me and me to U
I just never thought I would
See it through
(Blue, in Bacon, 2009, p. 153)

Unlocking the Tear Gates

I return to my bookshelf to take down a poetry book on comfort and healing that I frequently used in the nursing home when I facilitated poetry groups with residents. Pizer (1992) opens her poetry on grief and death by writing of the difficulty of men and boys in expressing their sorrow and grief. She writes of men who have not cried since they were small boys, taught instead to tough it out and act like men, while women were permitted gentleness, sadness, and tears. And I wonder aloud, when did girls stop crying openly? When did girls also begin to view tears as a sign of weakness and unacceptable vulnerability? While boys were being trained to be men, were African American girls simultaneously being conditioned to be strong Black women? Did the tears run dry as they/we transitioned from girlhood to Black womanhood? Did the tears run dry at the same time African American girls gave up wondering and wandering the beaten path into Black womanhood? Is the end of wondering and wandering the point when we become cloaked in the names of strong Black women and superwomen?

Each group member echoes the sentiment that they do not want to seem or to be vulnerable. I assure them that tears are not a sign of weakness and vulnerability. Vulnerability comes from the Latin word *vulnerabilis*, meaning "wounding." Included in this is *vulnerare*, which means "to wound" (Barnhart, 1995, p. 866). What does vulnerability call forth as African American adolescent girls or Black women? Is the "wounding" akin to leaving a fragile new life with skin peeled off and nerves exposed to the harsh elements of nature as it often feels? Or, perhaps, it is not the stripping off of skin but rather the casting off of unnecessary layers that are, in fact, too heavy to carry or bear any longer? This unburdening connects to suffering (Bacon, 2009). The Latin term for "suffer" or "sufferer" includes to "undergo" or "put under" (Barnhart, 1995, p. 775). Transformation occurs through suffering and grief. The transformation is driven by the necessity to dig up feelings as much as the necessity to "put under" burdens as described by Blue.

> Yelling, screaming, unsure
> I miss u with the love in me
> I'm crazy without your hugs...
> You in my life is what I lack-
> You make me mad
> Yelling, screaming, unsure
> You make me mad
> (Blue, in Bacon, 2009, p. 156)

As Blue digs up her feelings surrounding her grief and loss, she uncovers the means to bury her burdens. Writing her suffering allows Blue to be vulnerable. Through her poetry, Blue yells out for her mother's love and her hugs. As she reveals the pain of what her life now lacks, she begins to "put under" her sorrow. It is the vulnerability and suffering of one that becomes the pathway to connection for many.

With the casting off of layers and burdens, we uncover universal lived experiences from the particular.

Universal from the Particular

> ... I think poetry, or any writing, is but a reflection of the moment. The universal comes from the particular.
> (Giovanni, cited in Collins, 2000, pp. 268–269)

Lived experience is highly valued for women in the African American community, providing credibility, knowledge, and connection rather than distant statistics and irrelevant applications of the voices of others. As a result, many Black women scholars include their lived experiences and the experiences of other Black women to open up their methodologies. Black feminist epistemology recognizes standards used to assess knowledge or truth. This epistemology offers collective experiences along with accompanying world views against a historical backdrop (Collins, 2000). In my study, shared and collective wisdom has provided a bridge for African American girls to transition into Black womanhood (Bacon, 2009, 2017).

Wilderness: A Collective Poem

Dragged out into the death of night
Sounds of black women gasping for air
Choking back pain
Swallowing doses of hate
Digesting fear
Laughter from outsiders watching beneath closed eyelids
The parade of black women
    Limbs tangled between grasping hands wrapping
    themselves
Around their flesh | rapidly shredding dark skin
Brown gold orange hues bleed red
Fingers clawing at dignity
Scraping spirits
Fragmenting bodies from names
Fragmenting real from imagined sound from insane

Black women wandering like haints
Through the wilderness searching for dismembered body

parts
Searching for forgotten memories

Black women spitting up venom
Ejecting hatred
Regurgitating fear

Black women reaching for each other to remember
Remember remember find your way home
(Bacon, 2009, pp. 23–24)

Strong Black Women Crying
During Women's History month, I was asked to be a panel member for a local public school that designed a program for girls by honoring community "sheroes." And while the opportunity was provided to allow us to share our success stories, particularly in the way of academic achievement and career accomplishments, something unexpected unfolded that took a powerful turn. I experienced strong Black women and girls, collectively, without pretense or apology, crying in front of one another.

The girls who participated in the program that day unraveled their stories alongside ours. Our stories began to delve deeper than degrees and career choices into relationships and lived experiences. From behind the mask, we began to embrace our authentic selves and the authentic selves of one another as we shed our tears. By the end of each story shared in a room of 40–50 participants, there was not a dry eye.

Strong Black women can and do, in safe and sacred spaces, cry. That one-day workshop and panel discussion was so transformative because not only did each and every member feel permission to shed tears, but she also felt permission to embrace the others' pain. To stand for one another collectively offered a power that surpassed any individual emotional or physical strength. Truth leaked from tears that cleansed all stains of shame and secrecy, that not only excused but upheld vulnerability as a sacred expression. Each panelist, each staff member, each girl student who stood to "testify," did so with rawness and presence. That presence dissolved titles, false names, appearances, images, and lies that had been told about us and our existence as Black women and girls.

Hamilton's poem featured in Evelyn White's book, *Chain Chain Change: For Black Women in Abusive Relationships* (1995) invites the reader to face every pain, word, and deed that has ever hurt her, even when it brings about tears. She reminds Black women who have been hurt that the world will not fall apart because their tears are shed. Each Black woman is unique, beautiful, and deeply deserving of love and respect from herself, her partner, and society (White, 1995).

As I turn back to strong Black women who do cry, I am reminded of this affirmation with each story that was shared by the African American adolescent girls and Black women who spoke the day of the panel discussion. Each girl and woman who shared stories of success and triumph to basic survival was a "shero" by virtue of her Being.

And while the Poetic Eight was not present that day, many of their voices and own poetry writing reverberated with those who did speak then. It is these powerful revelations that return me to the charge/duty of the poet. Does the poet have a responsibility? If she feels an urgency to write to express her pain and to be heard, does she also feel compelled to express the pain of others who still have not found their own voices or have been so marginalized that they cannot speak? The collective voice has answered in response, yes; she does.

> ... before I'll be a slave I'll be dancing on my grave and go home to my soul and be free.
> (Walker, 1997)

Poetry offers an escape through imagination for women enslaved by their circumstances—women who rather than go to their graves in body and spirit write their way home to their souls to be free. With this declaration and imagination, instead of remaining in pain, women speak of laughing when they wanted to break down from their worlds being torn upside down. Within the group, they exude a sense of comfort in finding a source of love and strength in a circle of women friends. They share the pain of being brutalized by a partner but being told they could and would make it out of their relationships by a stranger who cared. Women that day unfold stories of attaining a college degree at fifty or defeating alcohol addiction when no one else believed that they could. They thank their mothers, who always believed in them. They honor the mother figures and mentors who succeeded before them and were role models. These Black women celebrate putting themselves through college, buying their own homes, and breaking down society's barriers to earn doctorates.

That day serves as another reminder of our collective strength and our work ahead as poets and writers. As stories unfold and the history of marginalization and voicelessness is revealed, tears are offered for ourselves, our mothers, and our ancestors. Although some of us never saw these young women before and others worked with them each day but had never heard these stories, all of us extended our arms to embrace and hold up the young women and girls coming behind us. There is the collective knowledge and understanding that strong Black women sound their cries to those who are willing to listen. And those cries have a powerful purpose. With this sounding, tears of loneliness, abandonment, and betrayal become tears of hope and healing.

According to Collins (2000), the hegemonic domain of power is firmly situated in its ability to distort and shape consciousness through the manipulation of images, ideologies, and ideas. Black feminist thought reclaims consciousness through an emphasis on the power of self-definition, leading to freedom and empowerment. Furthermore, in Black feminist thought consciousness is not believed to be fixed but rather continually evolving.

Behind the mask, a sisterhood exists that uplifts, upholds, and nurtures the experiences of girlhood and womanhood. Understanding and embracing this path and transition to Black womanhood offers the girlchild a guide, not only for wandering and wondering, but for vulnerability as a means of strength and self-expression. And as I return to my work with the Poetic Eight, I recognize that they must also unfold individually as well as collectively, to know what they must do for themselves when grief strikes again and they begin to feel overwhelmed. I begin this segment by posing the question, "Where will you go when you feel overwhelmed?"

Where Will You Go When Overwhelmed by Suffocating Emotion?

Where do you go once the tears have fallen and isolation comes back to your door? Where do you go as an African American adolescent girl poet on the brink of strong Black womanhood when you feel overwhelmed? Pizer (1992), who writes of healing and comfort, opens up the question of where you go when you are overwhelmed through her poem "Overwhelmed." As each girl who has carried the lived experience of grief from death, abandonment, loss, or pain continues this process, she must imagine her way home to her self.

Overwhelmed

> When I feel overwhelmed by destruction, Let me go down to the sea... Of limitless horizons and unknown universes... Until I am grown calm and strong once more. (Pizer, 1992, p. 39)

After reading "Overwhelmed" to the Poetic Eight, I ask them to write where they will go (metaphorically, metaphysically, or literally) for comfort and healing when they are feeling overwhelmed by their emotions or losses.

Walker (1997) writes about what she has gained in her life from her experiences, the people that have been placed along her path, her family, and her poetic journey. She ponders what she can give back to humanity as a mentor, big sister, and mother to all of the daughters born of her heart. And what Walker comes to recognize is that her greatest gift is her poetry. She writes her wisdom, advice, and compassion in her poem dedicated to loneliness, to courage, to sorrow, to strength, to despair.

In the poems below, the Poetic Eight offer their writing on being overwhelmed. The offerings of their poetry are their gifts to their sense of Being. Camille writes a poem for her thoughts as she enters into this activity. Her poem is a revelation of the power of her analytical mind and thoughtful silence to free herself from being overwhelmed when she is hurt and to stay calm.

Camille writes this poem to that place in her mind:

> Not knowing what to do
> Or where to go
> Getting lost in my thoughts...
> I go to a place in my mind...
> Let me stay in this place that keeps me calm.
> (Camille, in Bacon, 2009, p. 166)

Mishaps writes her poem to vulnerability. She offers an opening to a place inside her where she does not feel she has to hide her feelings or even her tears. And while she declares that she will not cry in front of others, her tears are where she runs to feel free when she is overwhelmed.

Mishaps writes to that place in her emotions where her tears safely hide:

> When I'm feeling overwhelmed I run straight
> To my tears or look through pictures, and
> Reminisce on past years
> I go to a place that you can't see and a place that you can't be
> I run directly inside of me...
> (Mishaps, in Bacon, 2009, p.166)

While Camille goes within her mind to feel free and Mishaps to her tears inside of herself, Blue ventures outside of her thoughts to escape feeling overwhelmed. Blue travels to nature to release her thoughts and feelings when overwhelmed. Like Pizer (1992), Blue retreats to the water to be cleansed by the waves that are powerful enough to wash away her sorrows and lose herself in what she loves.

Blue writes to that place outside of her mind:

> When I feel overwhelmed, I go outside of my mind to a beach with lots of overflowing water beyond [what] the eye can see...
> I would stop what I am doing and do something I love to do.
> For hours and hours until I don't feel overwhelmed anymore.

KiRe enters into the warmth of the kitchen when she is overwhelmed. Her reflection reveals her draw to creating community as her cooking "brings people together" when she is feeling overwhelmed. KiRe retreats to the place where everything comes out exactly as she intends and creates it to be in a shared space with her family.

KiRe writes to her happiness:

> I find sanity in the kitchen. Cooking makes me happy. For me, I sometimes [wish] my life was like a dish, because it seems whenever I cook, it comes out how I want it to, even when life doesn't do that. I also like cooking because it brings people together. No matter what the issues in my family are, it is forgotten once the food is smelled as soon as feet hit the kitchen floor.
> (KiRe, in Bacon, 2009, p. 167)

As the Poetic Eight begin to build bridges to their inner thoughts, writing, and feelings, they also build bridges to the feelings and experiences of one another. As the group unfolds through their writing where they will go and what they will do when they feel overwhelmed, the path of an adolescent poet is illuminated. As this path is made clear, Keisha reenters this space. Keisha returns to offer her story as an African American adolescent girl poet turned strong Black woman writer. Keisha shares that she does cry, with a purpose, and is not afraid to be vulnerable in her truth and in her writing.

The Return of The Poetic Daughter
For this portion of the journey, I leave my space as poet and educator to remember my previous journey as rhapsode and "other mother" when Keisha re-enters the poetic circle. Since the poetry group, Keisha has graduated from high school. Her senior year proves to be a productive one, and I receive reports from her teachers of her success. She is focused and ambitious and has become a role model for other students and her younger sister as she said that she would. I first contact her by email then by letter to congratulate her on her graduation and invite her to speak to my new poetry group. We speak by phone, and it is immediately apparent as she details her recent experiences with her writing, school, and job that she is no longer an African American adolescent girl but a strong Black woman. Keisha is now a Black woman writer and a teacher (through lived experience and example) who has maintained her sense of wonder and wander.

Keisha's poetry remains powerful and her voice certain. As I connect her previous lived experiences of her loss and pain to that of the members of the Poetic Eight, I know that my reading her poetry to the group will not do her work justice. Rather her story must be unfolded to the poetry group directly through her voice. I invite Keisha as a former adolescent girl poet who once sat in the space that members of the Poetic Eight now inhabit. As Keisha assumes her new role, she begins to help chart the waters through her words and writings for the Poetic Eight to travel behind her and to make their way to the shore.

Poetic Arrival
As I pull into the metro station, I finally notice her. Her physical body looks slight; I had not remembered that she was so short in stature. She appears thinner than the last time that I saw her, making her look almost fragile. But she is not. There is a depth in her eyes and a power in her voice that far exceeds her size and now matches her lived experiences.

When we finally arrive at the classroom where she will speak with the new poets, her mere presence calls for a response. She creates hushed tones followed by absolute silence when she walks into the room. Her presence will remain even after today when she will again move on. I will see her once more when I make other arrangements for her to join the group for a poetry program, but I will not know the next time she will resurface or where her homesteading path will lead her. Her homecoming path has led her back to this space to imprint her poetic footsteps and experiences as dust tracks on this road. She walks through this wilderness for the next group of poet warriors and griottes to follow her.

Keisha is as animated and humorous as she was in high school, and she carries the same sense of ownership (much like Mishaps and Blue) and commanding presence. She is also a natural leader in the room and is seemingly fearless in speaking her truths and sharing her voice. She follows my lead by sitting atop a desk to face the girls as she readies herself to read her poems and share her stories. Since graduating from high school, she has received an associate degree and is now returning to college for a bachelor's degree. She has a job she enjoys and a boyfriend she feels is supportive and treats her with respect, love, and dignity. She reminds the girls that they, too, can be anything and overcome anything and that she is a living testament to those very words.

Through Keisha's poetry there evolves a "co-responsive" truth born from the experience of listening for the girls and of being heard for Keisha. Keisha, who has never before seen or met this group, boldly steps from behind the mask to utter her truth in this sacred space without apology or indecision. She speaks with conviction; she reads with authority, and she offers her strength to the girls in my program through her poetry and her lived experience. And as the room falls silent, she reads her poem of the rape.

> It's not the type of thing a girl should go through. This guy took my body and tore it in two...Confusion on my face as I started to cry. Crossing my legs I wanted to die...
> (Keisha, in Bacon, 2009, p. 170)

Keisha then leaves them with a message that can be merged with many experiences surrounding violence, oppression, silence, and shame for girls and women. "I don't want anyone [girls and women] to be scared. Speak up. It's not your fault."

The girls are overcome by "truth as an experience with listening" (Levin, 1989, p. 136). Their eyes remain on hers; they speak words of agreement, sigh, and nod with an understanding that is not carried through words. As Keisha unfolds her poetry and truth, the Poetic Eight enter first into a space of epistemological silence. And through this truth and listening, there is an acknowledgement that we are responsible to one another and to humanity by what we hear. It is an experience that moves what is now an ontological silence (fulfilling silence) to voice and numbness to resonance.

The truths of poetry often reside in listening with an open heart and an active ear; the truths of poetry also reside in the writing and speaking of remembrances that move us from what is numb or not expressed to what is alive and felt. Our listening, poetry writing, and truth saying are interwoven and intertwined with one another's. Yet, we must first offer our silence in order to hear our own hearts and one another's. These weavings are filled with responsiveness, receptiveness, and care. Listening is also born of the wisdom and intuition of the feminine spirit that invites us all to return home to ourselves, our "I Ams."

Keisha's message of justice, voice, and self-acceptance will be further unconcealed by the Poetic Eight in the following sections. Moreover, in the next segment, I continue to unfold the process of writing, listening, and creating. Segment Seven begins with "My Real Name" as poetic identities and naming are uncovered and explored. Naming is the opening and interpreting of voice for the poets that deepens love, friendship, and justice. In subsequent segments, justice and divinity will occur in a space of fire and joy. As the sections unfold, the Poetic Eight's remembrances and connections allow them to enter into homecoming and homesteading with themselves and one another.

Section Seven

My Real Name

"My Real Name" is about uncovering the power to name who you really are through writing. As the process of naming unfolds, it nudges me to remember that phenomenology invites you into a space sometimes as shyly and quietly as the voices of Camille and Family who ask you, through the subtleties of their expression as well as their poetic silence, to listen actively, intuitively, with care, openness, a higher consciousness, and patience. However, there is deep enthusiasm by poetry group participants and me to bridge gaps, connect spaces and jump headfirst into the deep end of the phenomenological waters to discover and explore the bottom of the ocean floor and all that is living and growing in that space. Yet, this process gently reminds us all that some of what surfaces is not explored or dug up from beneath the ocean floor but sometimes floats to the surface, carried instead by a facial expression, a whisper, or a gentle drifting that leads you to a deeper poetic understanding of yourself and one another.

    This drifting is a reminder of the process of true poetic renderings. While this journey is about creation, re-creation, and movement, it is also about surrendering. There are times when the self-struggle of the participant writer is so painful, and the process so labored, that I must consciously fight the urge to thwart the writer's process by jumping into the water to drag her out. There are times when I have entered, waist deep or totally submerged in these phenomenological waters, as I have been led or called to do by their voices or their specific life circumstances. And there have been times that I have pushed against the current with my own restless movements that have pushed back and dragged me into even stronger tides. I permitted the poetic renderings to wash over and around me until, like Pizer (1992), I was not overwhelmed or anxious anymore. When calm and stillness came after being overwhelmed, so did the wherewithal to continue to observe and experience the breath of this poetic study and the rhythm of its unfolding (Bacon, 2009).

This uncovering and naming had its very own life, which offered the lived experience for members to be reborn again and again with each unconcealing, healing, storytelling, and writing. Self-struggle, re-creation, and poetic rebirth come through and by the grief and loss process in each member's own way.

In our poetry group it has come through laughing uproariously, crying sometimes inconsolably, writing, drawing, journaling, talking, checking in, embracing, being alone, and being together. It also comes through writing poetic calls and responses to each other, poetry discussions, and writing workshops; but mostly it comes through the courage to write and to share individual and collective stories and the courage to hear what is and is not spoken. In this segment, to respect the courageous naming of the poets, I choose to stay with their original work rather than rely on outside sources.

Uncovering the Naming

There are many collective lived and poetic experiences in the group; yet, uncovering the power to name who you are through poetry writing is a distinctively individual and unique experience. Mishaps' piece "I Don't Know What I Need" resonates with KiRe because of its individual nature. Moreover, the poem sets forth a charge for/to the listener to see behind the mask to the experiences of the writer as she unfolds her own personal journey, feelings, and questions of "I Am." Following Mishaps' poem, KiRe offers her voice to this space as a rhapsode in response to Mishaps' unconcealing and exploration of her real name. As Mishaps begins her journey, finding the anam cara in her self and receiving it by others creates self-struggle.

> I don't need
> What I need
>
> > I don't need Nobody- I think!
> > I hope! I won't be happy until
> > I'm all alone then how will I cope
> > I don't need friendz or fam menz or
> > Manz, goonz with empathy and
> > I damn sure don't need your sympathy...
>
> Maybe I don't know what I need.
> (Mishaps, in Bacon, 2009, p. 174)

The following is KiRe's poetic response to Mishaps' poem "I Don't Know What I Need."

> I hate when people say "I know how you feel"
> Because they don't
> Nobody knows, I DON'T EVEN KNOW
> Fantasies clash with reality
> Memories collide with tomorrow...
> This simple complexity is peeling the layers of my stability, but nobody understands don't tell me you know how I feel
> I HATE THAT!! Or maybe I hate that someone could understand me...
> When I don't even understand myself
> (KiRe, in Bacon, 2009, pp. 174–175)

Mishaps' story has been one of a strong Black woman, much like the women in Section Four, who have exclusively offered support, leadership, and consolement to others. In the past, Mishaps has not allowed herself to receive support from others or to be in reciprocal relationships. As she unravels her feelings and declarations of what she does not need, she begins to uncover another layer of her poetic identity (Bacon, 2009). Beneath the surface is a layer of vulnerability and questioning expressed through the exclamation, "I don't need Nobody-I think!"

Mishaps' initial denial of her needs and of her vulnerability, followed by her self-inquiry, allow her to journey to the inbetween spaces of strong Black womanhood to arrive at the end-place of homesteading in acceptance and belonging. When Mishaps states "I don't need friendz or fam menz or manz," she reveals a place within herself that is still raw and fragile. Mishaps' lived experiences as a daughter of domestic violence, a motherless daughter, and a surrogate mother for her younger siblings have taught her that in order to survive she must not ask or depend on anyone outside of herself (Bacon, 2009; Williams, 2008).

Yet, as Mishaps begins to dig up her concealed emotions through her poetry, her needs to connect and to belong begin to surface. How can she reconcile the need to conceal her feelings to survive her pain and the need to connect and be fully alive? How do you live and breathe when your needs are at odds with each other?

Through Mishaps' poetry she confronts her pain and her loss as she confronts her father and God: "But how do I explain this to the men who... Took you away... I can't scream at him cuz he hears... But never has anything to say." In her poetry, Mishaps can scream at her father, who does not hear her when she speaks, and even scream at God, who did not answer her prayers and spare her mother's life. As Mishaps writes her declarations, questions, and screams, she enters into a new poetic consciousness, revealing "Maybe I don't know what I need."

The Poetic Eight connects with Mishaps through their compassion and understanding. However, KiRe connects to Mishaps' poem by first acknowledging that no one else can fully understand your grief but you. Even though many members of the group have struggled with feelings of grief and loss, each girl's lived experience and journey to healing and acceptance is her own. Therefore, KiRe's poetic interpretation and response to Mishaps' poem is brought forth not through a shared lived experience but through her exclamation, "I hate when people say I know how you feel Because they don't..."

And while KiRe's writing affirms the uniqueness of individual voices and lived experiences, she, too, uncovers another layer of truth brought forth by vulnerability. KiRe's poetry writing acknowledges "Or maybe I hate that someone could understand me." Her poetic questioning leads me to ponder: In our humanness, are we more afraid of connecting with and being understood by others than being rejected by them?

Today My Name Is
While it is the girls' voices and writings that lead us to themes and naming(s), their uncovering(s) were further prompted by such questions as, "Who am I?" "What do I name myself?" "Is what I name myself what others name me?" Understanding themselves and one another begins with the process of uncovering their name(s). As a group, we read "My Real Name," a poem by Noel (Writerscorps, 2003, p. 46) that begins: "Today my name is colorful... Yesterday my name was... Tomorrow my name will be...." I asked that we each read a line from the poem. After each member read a line, enabling her to have her voice heard, I asked the group to say the line that resonated with them personally.

The reading opens with Mishaps calling out with conviction, "Yesterday my name was dead souls." As we move around the room, each poet seems to fall exactly in place with the line that she needs to read in that moment (even before they are asked to call out the line that has meaning for them). Blue follows with "Tomorrow my name will be lively spirits." Queen of Hearts roars "My friends think my name is fire." Divine Diva whispers "My parents think my name is symphony." Lenash closes with "Secretly I know my name is anything I want it to be." After we complete the reading, I ask each poet to call out another line of her choosing. Mishaps and Lenash select the same opening and closing lines of the poem that they read at the beginning of the activity.

Lively Spirits: Urgent Naming
As we move into the next activity, each adolescent girl receives a copy of the poem with the first line "Today may name is colorful" removed. I ask them to make the original poem their own by completing the first line for themselves: "Today my name is…" Following "today," they are invited to create and add a self-selected name for "yesterday" and "tomorrow" (Bacon, 2009). I share that their names can be anything that they choose or want them to be—from a color to a feeling, sound, season, thought, or idea (Bacon, 2009). As they create their names, I invite them to reflect on feelings of "I Was, I Am," and "I Will Be."

There seems to be a feeling of restlessness in the room as they reflect, engage, discuss, or appear to avoid discussing their naming (turning to look out of the window, glancing at a cell phone, chatting to their neighbors or to me). Levin (1989) reminds us that there are many different ways for us to be with, relate to, or be in situations and experiences in our lives. Moreover, we perceive through a variety of channels (tactile, auditory, emotional, intellectual), orientations (curiosity, analytical, passive), perspectives (glancing sideways, looking straight ahead), and degrees of intensity (focused, staring, touching lightly, listening excitedly) as well as self-awareness.

Almost ten minutes have now passed since we started (although to me, and maybe to some of the others, it feels like thirty). I repeat the last line of the poem out loud, "Secretly I know my name is anything that I want my name to be." I ask the participants to write "I want my name to be…" followed by a word that names them as well as the poem. They begin to speak out names that they could have been given at birth or playfully ask and tease, "Do I look like a __?" while laughing. "Push yourselves to be abstract," I encourage as they continue to mull over and compare the literal names they might use or are familiar with. "Today my name is," I repeat. I then inquire, "What do you want it to be?," and the activity begins to unfold. But as I probe, I begin to feel a sense of urgency (Bacon, 2009).

Why aren't they mounting this hurdle? I am expecting them to dive in with reckless abandon but instead feel confronted by their naming of the obvious or expected. How is this uncovering the power of writing that has guided my study of being and naming? I begin slowly calling out words from the poem: "fire, secretly, lively spirits." Creating connections in this naming to their flow and reflections of I was, I am, I will be. Chatter and laughter begin until I firmly redirect them to the page; my sense of urgency is growing in intensity. This is not as I had imagined the process to unfold as I was carefully creating, planning, and organizing each activity. The realization comes to me: I am frustrated. Digging a little deeper, I realize it is more than frustration; there is concern as I question why they cannot answer how they would name themselves or what their real names are. Have I failed them? What is more, if they cannot name themselves, how do I know the truth in my names and identities (educator, poet/writer, phenomenologist researcher, arts activist)?

In spite of my phenomenological desire for gentle unfolding, I am attached to the outcome of this activity. Moreover, in not wanting others (including me) to impose names on my participants, I am ironically tempted to demand that they (in order to claim their emancipation) label themselves, and label themselves in a certain way. I once again hear the voice of Heidegger, "Teaching is more difficult than learning... because what teaching calls for is this: to let learn" (Heidegger, as cited in Hultgren, 1995, p. 371).

There are times when we are engaged with acute or heightened awareness and participation, and other times when we are distant, detached, or simply absent-minded. Levin (1989) shares a reflection of a psychotherapist who recognizes that he does not always follow his own process in order to be able to "be there for the other person" (p. 18). I am reminded again, through this experience of naming, of the need to listen actively to the different voices (spoken, unspoken, emotional, intellectual, and physical) to be able to follow as well as lead. Moreover, the process of speaking, reflecting silently, fidgeting, drifting, glancing, engaging, wandering, laughing, smiling, imagining and questioning are the unfoldings of their, and my, many names.

Symphony
With these revelations, my shoulders become more relaxed. I begin to shift my posture to shrug off the burden of outcomes and expectations. And with the opening of the next activity, we wonder and wander as led by our own processes and imaginations.

Across the table, I have scattered the index cards with the names "colorful," "dead souls," "lively spirits," "fire," "burden," "symphony" and "secretly" from the poem. As I take a step back, they are invited to step to the front to pick up a brightly colored index card with the name from the poem that "belongs" to them. As they come to the table, they look excitedly at the names. Some of the girls again become pensive and quiet, while others talk, giggle. and compare ideas.

Each poet takes the card that she considers to be a symbol of her naming and a part of her identity, soul, or her gift. Divine Diva claims the name of Burden, traced back to her feelings of being unwanted and unexpected as unfolded previously in Section Four. Camille steps into the name of Secretly, connecting with her silence. Mishaps declares her name to be Dead Souls, acknowledging her numbness from the death of her mother. Blue embraces the name Fire and her voice of passion. Queen of Hearts names herself Colorful as she embraces her personality and feeling that her color is gold, which she sees as good luck. Lenash names herself Symphony as she declares her lived experiences playing in harmony with most of those around her in her life. And KiRe announces her animation and enthusiasm by selecting the name Lively Spirits. Once she has selected one of her many names, I invite each girl to explore creating her own "My Real Name" poem. Through the declaration, a shift begins to occur.

Everything

As we continue with naming, we follow "My Real Name" to return to the Poetic Eight's initial individual naming through their chosen pen names. Following the first activity, reflections seem to deepen as each member shares her feelings surrounding the meaning of her name. As the unfolding(s) occur, the adolescent girls' writings lead them to everything from where they come from to who they were, are, and will be.

> Today my name is everything
> Yesterday my name was nothing but now, that solemn silence
> Is now blasting boisterously...
> (KiRe, in Bacon, 2009, p. 181)

KiRe is often thought of as the lighthearted one in the group because she keeps people smiling and laughing. She reveals there were times when she felt she could not tell people if she wasn't "feeling good," or that it was her job to make people happy (even at her own expense). Yet, what she learns about herself through her writing and naming is that "I am truly a lot happier than even I thought I was." The happiness she declares and affirms is emerging from a deeper self that is not based on others' perceptions or feelings about her (although she shares one thing that continues to make her happy and feel good is helping others, like many of the other girls in the group). At this point in her naming, she realizes that when she works on making herself happy, her happiness is genuine. She now declares with conviction as a "Lively Spirit" that if "you're mad be mad. It is okay to express it and to cry and if you're happy be happy but not for others you don't have to pretend to be or feel something that you don't." In embracing all of her emotions, she declares her name today is "Everything."

My Real Name

Today my name is Blue Jay
Tomorrow my name will be Fire
My friends think my name is Thunder
The police think my name is sweet
My parents think my name is lovely
Secretly I know my name is black power
Or anything I want it to be.
(Blue, in Bacon, 2009, pp.182–183)

Blue originally selected her pen name to describe her emotions after the loss of her mother. Yet, toward the end of the program, Blue offers a different interpretation of her name. "[It is] something to describe me but not necessarily saying that I'm blue... but it's saying... blue is a normal color...I don't feel the same way as I felt before I came in here because the poetry group helped me with my feelings and emotions." And with the new meaning of her naming, she declares she will keep her pen name. Blue further unfolds her own identity through her writings on her life and her goals that unfold in spite of the pain she has endured. Blue, like the "Blue Jay" of her name for today in "My Real Name," can still fly. Blue is also drawn to unfolding her naming and poetic identity through her desire and ability to help others as she shares in her poetic reflection "My Life Starts with a Word."

My Life Starts with a Word
A word of justice
That I have always wanted to practice
My life cries law
My duty is to help, good and bad...

> My life, my life, my goal
> (Blue, in Bacon, 2009, p.183)

Queen of Hearts names herself "Colorful" (for her animated presentation and personality and excitement for life). In addition to the other girls such as Blue, KiRe, and Mishaps, she offers part of her naming through the lens of others and her ability to help people, listen, and "make" them feel better about themselves. I wonder, as they unfold their naming through their ability to help and take care of others, at what point could "helping you hurt me" as unfolded by many of the strong Black women in Section Four? Queen of Hearts further unfolds her naming in her reflection and discussion.

Colorful

> My pen name was Queen of Hearts. I've come up with that because you know when people are upset. Like I'm always there to help them out. I'm always there to help them with their hearts. To fix it. So, I call myself the Queen of Hearts. [It's] something that I want to do. I want to help people. Maybe become a psychologist.

However, when I ask her how she mends her own heart she responds:

> Sometimes I try not to make as many mistakes as I can. I try not to rush many things. Try to keep everything real. I don't want all that emotion stuff but when it comes down to it if I have to cry I will cry. I have a book for my thoughts, a book for poetry (referring to the notebooks I gave to each student during the first poetry group meeting). When I'm writing my poems it's from a different experience. Not the troubles I would write in my thoughts. I think I want to write more about how we have evolved ever since this program has started. When I read my poems to y'all it's like, 'Oh snap I really like this!' I want to minor in creative writing. I name myself as a poet and as a writer.

Through her naming and own poetic revealing she invites the listener to take a deeper glance past the surface into her heart.

Burden

> A burden of those who didn't expect me Forever wondering
> am I loved by my family
> Today my name is heart... I want my name to be loved-
> (Divine Diva, in Bacon, 2009, p.185)

Uncovering the power to name allows a clearing from "Burden" for Divine Diva. Divine Diva moves from her selection of the name "Burden" to unfolding the creation of her pen name. "I just thought of it because I went to my aunt's church... They had this conference Divine Divas... for young women. My grandma also calls me that. It's my alter ego. Divine means that I'm God's child and Diva that I can do what I set my mind to."

> Today my name is pain on top of fire...
> Yesterday my name was boulder...
> Tomorrow my name will be a reflection of the future...
> (Mishaps, in Bacon, 2009, p, 185)

For Mishaps, it is her process of suffering that allows her to "put under" her first naming of "Dead Souls" to create a living name of pain, fire, and reflection (Barnhart, 1995, p. 775). "I picked the name Mishaps because of all the bad things that happened: Drama, tragedy, a world of pain, a world of Mishaps." Mishaps returns to her naming, through her pen name while reflecting on its creation.

> I mean I feel better when I'm here. I feel good. I feel relieved. I feel stressless. I feel real good. I mean I probably would think about changing the name. But then I also have to think about that after I leave this room, it's always going to be the same out there and that's what my name represents. So, I wouldn't change it. I think I'm going to find things that are always going to make me feel that way because there are always too many goodbyes and not enough hellos. People come in your life but more of them leave than stay. I think that's the hardest part for me.

Mishaps makes the distinction between safety, belonging, and acceptance in this sacred poetic space versus the outside world. The poetry group provides a place for Mishaps and the other girls to step from behind the mask to begin to reveal their true poetic identities, which encompass their vulnerability, creativity, empowerment, and voices (Collins, 2000). In our discussion, Mishaps acknowledges that our time together is now limited. The poetry group will soon be ending and Mishaps, Queen of Hearts, and KiRe will be graduating high school.

While Mishaps expresses great enthusiasm over her graduation, the close of the poetry group and her senior year require that she once again say goodbye to people she has come to deeply care for and who care deeply for her. In order to say goodbye, will Mishaps need to detach herself again from her feelings and her loss? Without Mishaps' vulnerability, her heart would not have been made accessible to the group or, most important, to her. Mishaps declares that the outside world, for her, will always be filled with unfortunate circumstances and mishaps. Yet, she has uncovered the power to name herself and maintains her power through her choice to continue to use her original pen name.

Unfolding Who I Am
The Poetic Eight's power to uncover who they really are through their writing allows them to call forth the names from where they came and share the importance of their cultures and heritage. They embrace who they were, who there are and who they will be. As they continue to uncover the power to name themselves, we venture through the wilderness by returning to their homecoming (where they are from). Homecoming requires a return to a place, even if the stay there is temporary. Homecoming allows a connection to be made with those who still reside there, those who have departed, with our memories, current and past selves (Casey, 1993; Bacon, 2009).

Revisiting this space (physically or poetically) can bring about closure and peace with the past and beckon us to journey to a new space through homesteading that will be our future home-place. However, connecting to our cultural legacies and heritage through writing also provides the opening for co-habitancy between homecoming and homesteading by means of a culturally responsive poetic co-existence between contemporaries and ancestors, or those who remain and those who have departed (Bacon, 2009).

Divine Diva's story is set against the backdrop of her family's lived experiences in the Deep South. Her family's cultural and historical truths inspired her to write pieces about slavery, lynching, Jim Crow, psychological and physical brutality, and other atrocities inflicted on African Americans throughout history. Today, as the keeper of culture and legacy, she begins with her homecoming through sharing her contemporary, culturally responsive poetry about growing up in the District of Columbia in "2 Words D.C." She writes, "The Cap, the home of Go-Go Chocolate City...Chillin at Ben's Chili Bowl...A mural Mandela, Bob Marley, Malcolm X, Dr. King..." (Divine Diva, in Bacon, 2009, p. 188).

Freire (1994), in *Pedagogy of Hope*, declares that his work was "Written in rage and love, without which there is no hope" (p. 4). Divine Diva and Lenash offer their writings and voices in rage and love from which hope and connection are brought forth in their poems "2 Words D.C.," "Nigerian Woman," "This is My Hair," and "U Say." In "2 Words D.C.," Divine Diva shares her cultural experiences growing up in the District of Columbia. She remembers the historic sites of Washington, D.C. through "Chillin at Ben's Chili Bowl" to the influences of such powerful national leaders as Dr. Martin Luther King and Minister Malcolm X.

Through cultural murals in Washington, D.C., Divine Diva also is connected to the global legacies and works of Nelson Mandela and Bob Marley. While Divine Diva's poem is a celebration of culture and homecoming, she further unfolds the struggles with violence and oppression that are faced within the community. "But gunshots would flare When up came the darkness..." And through writing with truth, love, hope, and cultural pride, Divine Diva embraces and integrates the ancient with the contemporary as a place of homecoming and homesteading. "[D.C.] One of my favorite places in the world...I want my friends to come & see..."

Lenash's culturally responsive poetry begins with her homecoming to Nigeria to unfold her lived experiences and those of her family living within the shackles and confines of poverty, oppression, and domination. She further writes of Nigeria and the intersections of Nigerian and American culture, hence deepening her poetic naming. As she writes of her homecoming, she creates a clearing to her homesteading by proudly acknowledging, declaring, and claiming her heritage and passage into womanhood in her poem "Nigerian Woman."

In Nigerian Woman (inspired by Maya Angelou's [1994] "Phenomenal Woman"), Lenash writes, "It's my heritage And so... it is me A brown skin woman With Nigerian hair And no other sign that I care..."

Lenash unfolds,

> Just because I don't know my Nigerian speech
> Doesn't mean that my head is too high to reach.

> Trust, I am what you do not perceive...
> Just because on the out[side] I'm not in my African clothes
> And the only way you see I'm Nigerian is through my nose...
> Don't doubt that I am, a Nigerian, woman.
> (Lenash, in Bacon, 2009, pp. 189–190)

In this poem, Lenash exists in a place of co-habitancy wrapped in Nigerian and American naming(s), identities, lived experiences, perceptions, and expectations. Her American homesteading is a place that is void of the speech, dialect, or languages of her Nigerian culture. It is also void of the dress and the gender roles of her Nigerian foremothers. And while she does not adorn a dashiki or maintain the tradition of toiling for a husband or children, preparing goat and rice diners, or washing and folding clothes by hand, she cautions others not to rename her identity as she is still a Nigerian woman. Americans and Nigerians often do not "perceive" Lenash's identity as African, although she writes her Nigerian heritage can be seen in her natural hair (texture): "With Nigerian hair... And no other sign that I care." While the women who are more assimilated or Americanized choose to straighten their hair, the women who embrace their full Nigerian identity often braid their hair. Through Lenash's poetry, it is unfolded that her hairstyle (neither straightened nor braided) represents a lack of caring about her culture and her appearance according to others. This perception is further expanded upon by Lenash in her poem "This is My Hair."

There is tension co-existing in the space of homecoming and homesteading as Lenash proudly claims the Nigerian American heritage that is shared between contemporary and ancient practices and life circumstances. In this tension, Lenash also offers the voice of resistance to colonization and domination through her writing. "The white man putting them down and saying it's for the best..." she writes in reference to the raping of land, resources, homes, and cultures of African people during colonization and post-colonization (Hilliard, 1998; Walker, in Graham, 1997). Lenash offers a counter-narrative to oppression (Collins, 2000) in her poem by challenging a class system that places greater value on her existence than her family's because she is deemed to be "Worth more than African siblings who are poorer." To this affront, she responds with defiance and a voice of solidarity, "Trust, I am what you do not perceive... Don't doubt that I am, a Nigerian, woman."

Unlike Lenash's homecoming, the meaning of Camille's homecoming is deciphered through what is not written in her poem. Camille takes us through her homecoming to Southern California where memories reside of friendships of the soul (anam cara) and the joy of her early years. Her homecoming is brought forth through memories of the first six years of her life, wrapped safely beneath the warmth of the California sun. As she first reads of her homecoming, her voice is a distant and faint whisper. She is invited to return home again with another reading in order to allow her voice to become more audible. With the next sounding, her voice is heightened and carries throughout the room, allowing her to be fully heard and to remember.

> On the other side of the country
> On the border of the Atlantic ocean...
> That's where I'm from
> Southern California...
> The place that, I miss
> That's where I'm from.
> (Camille, in Bacon, 2009, p. 192)

Camille's homecoming offers the joy of life that is carefree, warm, and fulfilling. In group discussions, she frequently references her childhood best friends and her longing for them. With her childhood best friends, Camille shares, she has a voice. Throughout the poetry program, Camille struggles with being shy, reading her poetry and writing from beneath the surface. Perhaps, this unfolding in her poem of the first six years of life represents the simplicity of "I Am." Does Camille's poem represent a place and a time that requires no explanation or meaning? And as Camille shares the joy of playing with her best friends in a place where she "had a fun life," she offers no voice to what she misses outside of "the place." Camille, who was adopted after her sixth year and moved to the East Coast, offers no indication or recollection of her feelings or memories after age six in her writing. Could it be that the only memories Camille needs to transition from homecoming to homesteading are what she offers on the surface of her writing? What poetic wisdom resides there?

Poetic Wisdom
The majority of the girls in my study created and claimed their identities and names in their works and writing comfortably and naturally as African American adolescent girl poets who saw

themselves as powerful in their words and in their space(s)—the poetry group, school, and society. For some members, writing is not as much of a way of uncovering power as it is a way of declaring, expressing, and affirming it for themselves and others. They are young African American women who have not had their wandering and wondering preempted by the dominant culture that forced naming of race, gender, class, ability or age upon them (Carroll, 1997; Sewell, 2006). However, many come into this space of power and voice with their understandings and lived experiences as daughters of Black women who have endured multiple oppressions, from which they perished or were otherwise left voiceless, physically or emotionally.

The Voice of Resistance
The power that they sought as African American adolescent girls and daughters of Black women, declaring "I Come From," "I Am" and "My Real Name," was granted through rewriting their lives, telling their stories and the stories of their mothers and loved ones (Bacon, 2009; Writerscorps, 2003). Uncovering the power to name who they really are through their writing is the journey from homecoming to (a self-created) homesteading.

Members of the Poetic Eight offer their voices by writing poetry, which resembles many of the descriptions and feelings of adolescent poets in *City of One* (DeDonato, 2004) and *Paint Me Like I Am* (Writerscorps, 2003). They define poetry for themselves as, "the best way to express yourself, your thoughts, emotions, and how you feel," as they further reveal their own naming and power. With this uncovering, Divine Diva, as the historical storyteller and griotte of the group, declares that "Poetry is saying how you feel [and] speaking and telling stories for people that can't tell stories or [are] afraid to tell stories." Each poet offers her voice to African and African American poetic culture and family through her writing, storytelling, homecoming and homesteading. KiRe also pays tribute to the wisdom and "knowing" offered and embodied in the "elders."

Driven by "the love of wisdom" and assertion of Aristotle that "All men by nature desire to know" (Babich, 2006, p. 3), my thoughts return to the knowing that African American and Black women and girl poets personify and express through their creations. Rather than experience a desire, as stated by Aristotle, as all men "desire to know," the African American adolescent girls and Black women in my study, honor their knowing and their lived experiences on their terms and in their own language through their writings. "For language is the most delicate and thus the most susceptible vibration…" (Heidegger, 1969, p. 38). The delicate vibration created by language is linked to emancipation (Freire, 1994). This form of emancipation comes, for many Black women and girls, through knowing, understanding, and acknowledging historical, societal, collective, and personal pasts.

By understanding suffering, struggle, and the history of oppression, these young poets' words are also laced with feelings of hope. There is a need to dream and imagine something greater, something different and something better than what society has defined. Without hope, we cannot see our way through struggle and instead become fatigued, overwhelmed, or immobilized. When we dare to fight through our poetic expressions and voices, and truly believe in the possibility of change we are seeking to resurrect, there is power in the truth that we are speaking (Freire, 1994).

Courage, resilience, and strength are derived from our legacies, roots, and heritage as we acknowledge the degradation of the oppressive experiences of the past and present alongside the dignity, wisdom, and grace of ancestors, elders, mothers, mother figures and ourselves. Divine Diva unconceals her voice of resistance and connection to legacy in "U Say."

> U say I'm not gonna amount to nothin'
> All I can say is u must be on something
> I can do what ever I want to do
> What I set my mind to…
>
> I come from kings & queens who were royalty
> Tell me how far back can u go [in] ur family tree
> (Divine Diva, in Bacon, 2009, pp. 196–197)

Margaret Walker's essays from 1932–1992 echo a voice of ancient foremothers as Divine Diva declares her freedom and resistance and affirms Black womanhood through writing. She asserts that, if nowhere else, in her thoughts and in her mind, she is completely free. And that freedom, she declares, for many African Americans must be expressed in her writing. "As a woman, I have come through the fires of hell because I am a black woman, because I am poor, because I live here in America, and because I am determined to be both a creative artist and maintain my inner integrity and my instinctive need to be free" (Walker, in Graham, 1997, p. 5).

Queen of Heart's journey concludes this segment as she embarks on her homecoming by unconcealing her poetic identity from beyond the mask to growing freedom. Queen of Heart's journey within offers the discovery of her true self. As she opens "new doors to new beginnings," her homesteading begins. She writes, "I am from a chapter of new beginnings…"

Queen of Hearts shares in her previous discussions and reflections that she wants to write about the progress she has made since the poetry group began. Her writings in "Where I'm From?!" offer insight into the hard work that she has put forth to develop not only as a writer but as a young woman who is free from others' perceptions and expectations. While Queen of Hearts once wrote that her purpose was to help others with their emotions, she now writes that there will be "No more masks to tame your emotions…" Like KiRe, Queen of Hearts is often the most animated and enthusiastic member of the group. She frequently makes others laugh or smile and has shared that her aim is to make others feel better. Yet, as the group continues, she seems to have uncovered the power to express her own emotions as she moves to this new beginning of homesteading with strength and certainty.

New Beginnings and Renewal

As the Poetic Eight members embrace where they have come from and where they are going, they begin to explore new beginnings and renewal. The idea of new beginnings and renewal is connected to our entering into the season of spring. An activity was originally scheduled to be designed and facilitated by Family around spring (her chosen topic). However, she was unable to create or attend the group meeting at that time, so I designed and facilitated an activity that would still allow her topic to be honored (while connecting it to previous themes such as grief, loss, and naming).

As I begin the facilitation process, I ask each member to think of the season fall (as it relates to the past). With this imagining, they are asked to think of what they would like to fall away (a thing, quality, circumstance/situation, characteristic) and what they would like to spring into (a new beginning) or what they would like to invite, grow, bud, or blossom (a quality, dream, goal, situation, circumstance, characteristic). As we connect the seasons, not just of the year but of life and feelings, each member is asked to connect again to her naming and her past, present, and future by writing who she was when she first came to the program, who she is now (as she declares or questions "I Am") and who she desires to become. The power to uncover and claim their poetic selves and identities opens up with reflections, truths and declarations before they take on the life of the poems that further share their stories and lived experiences. Mishaps, as she has through Section Four on grief, leads the way to what is to fall away in order to bury her suffocation and invite her renewal and rebirth.

> To fall away: My grief, pain and confusion
> To invite: Affection, happiness, change, music and knowledge
>
> I was a bitter person. I was upset all the time. Crying all the time. I don't like to let people know it or show it a lot. Cause I don't know I think people use that as a weakness. Most people I know. I was angry... I was hurt...
>
> I am I still am but not as much. And then coming in here I became more open. I always wanted to talk coming in here... I was happy to talk. Willing to talk. That changed my talking a lot. I used to talk a lot when my mother was here but then I stopped. Coming in here it's like it filled a piece of my heart in. Now I can use that piece.
>
> I will be powerful. I will be a better me.

Through Mishaps' reflections and poetry, she further reveals the process of "I Am" with unflinching honesty. In her poetry she unfolds the stages of her grief and loss, beginning with her feelings of anger and hopelessness, to arrive at feeling, "I am happy I am whole." As she enters into the phase of what she will be, she writes her dreams and goals. "I will broaden my horizon" and "I will be a doctor, I might even be a nurse." As Mishaps shares her feelings and desires, she comes to a place in homesteading that begins to reveal an integrated acceptance of herself when she writes, "I will be me for better and for worse" (Bacon, 2009; Turner & Helms, 1991).

Camille quietly comes into this space to offer her reflections and declaration.

> What I want to fall away is my lack of confidence. I shouldn't care what people may say I should just forget about it. I mainly want my shyness to fall away because it keeps [me] from things often.

> I want to invite a new Camille one that will throw away the old one and never let it come back because she enjoys it (the life of the new Camille).
>
> I was nervous I am a little shy I will be more outgoing
> I am a shy person Keeping to myself Many hours of the day
> Holding my head down So won't think people are staring
> Keeping my voice low To certain people I've been like this for a while now
> Don't know why Always meeting new people Or reuniting with those that
> Knew me when I was younger I break out of it with close friends
> But never with anyone else I am a shy person But will be more outgoing
> (Camille, reflection in Bacon, 2009, p. 201)

Camille unfolds her "I Am" through her reflections of what she wants to fall away and what she wants to invite. She offers her "I Am" through her cultural legacy as "Queen of the Nile" and the survivor of the slaughter of slaves. Camille's identities unfold as the daughter of a minister, "I am a preachers daughter," to the confidante of her mother, "I am my mothers weeper." She reveals through her many identities an emerging voice of an adolescent girl who was once "with very little to say" and "lets life pass me by." As she uncovers her voice, new beginnings of hope and a new level of glory emerge: "I am the one who hopes to be glory bound." Through her declarations, reflections, and poetry, Camille claims her "I Am" as "a person who thinks you'll love me for me."

Although Family did not attend that day, when she returned to the group she offered her voice and reflections.

> I was shy when I first came here. I did not share my inner me like everybody else.
>
> Now I am still working on speaking in front of a big crowd because I get [stage fright] right but I am getting over it now (Family's "stage fright" is one of the reasons she was not able to facilitate).

I will be one day an outspoke[n] person who will present her stuff in front of a big crowd and not [stutter].

Family offers her voice of self-acceptance through a poem of "I Am" that reveals that in spite of what she may seek to change (speaking in front of large crowds), she remains "...all that I want to be." Joy unfolds for Family when she enters into self-reflection and affirmation. "I have within me... honesty, hope, dreams, to reach to a high standard [and] peace." Although she continues to long for the love and connection to her family of origin, she still manages to begin to rewrite her grief and uncover her power. "When I am down in the dumps I always know a way to bring myself up."

Each member of the Poetic Eight through her poetry and declarations affirms her sense of self-love and worth through the poetic mirror as she embraces her vulnerability with truth and new insight.

Queen of Hearts continues to unfold her poetic names as she reveals her hopes for the future, goals and identities that are as diverse and different as each pizza topping. She claims her many names from "freedom writer... Or Black Panther" to "Oprah Winfrey or Bill Gates." As she unfolds her "I Am," she further reveals that no matter what the outcome of her goals and choices will be, she will "keep myself going" when she once unfolded her purpose was to live for others.

Divine Diva unfolds her voice and sense of self-acceptance as "I Am" through her written reflections and declarations

> What I want to fall away is the drama I deal with all the time. I want to get rid of the thoughts that everything's my fault
>
> What I want to grow is my determination to be known in the world.
>
> I was...
> I was the girl who had a lot to say
> But was afraid of what others said about me.
> Was my hair right? Will they talk about my clothes or shoes? It mattered to me if I had a boyfriend or not. Because I look like the only girl w/o a boyfriend. I didn't feel comfortable with most of my friends because, I'm not all skinny like them. I was disgusted at the way my body was.

I am...
Now confident in myself & ready to try to be a teenager. I'm proud that I have curves and that I don't look like everyone else... I'm a girl who isn't afraid to speak her mind.

I will be ...
Whatever I choose to be... I want to be a singer, dancer, actress, director, producer, activist, mentor, & own my own businesses.
(Divine Diva, in Bacon, 2009, p. 204)

Divine Diva shares through her poetry, reflections, and discussions her struggles with self-acceptance, image, and belonging. She writes about feeling like a burden to her family and the need to be a "good girl." Through her writing she shares her fears: "I was the girl who had a lot to say. But was afraid of what others said about me." Divine Diva also questions her physical appearance in her writing: "Was my hair right?" "Will they talk about my clothes or shoes?"

I once wondered will Divine Diva give herself the permission to break free from the oppressive language, labels, and images that silence her voice. And as Divine Diva uncovers the power to name who she really is, she answers in the affirmative. As Divine Diva enters into the phase of "I Am," she writes from "I was disgusted at the way my body was" to "I'm proud that I have curves and that I don't look like everyone else..." Moreover, as Divine Diva uncovers that she is "a girl who isn't afraid to speak her mind" she boldly declares, "I will be whatever I choose to be."

KiRe, who is the daughter of ministers, talks about a turning point in her life toward personal truth. Like Blue, Mishaps, and many of the other girls in the group, she feels that she has learned the most from her mother. She has learned "I Am" as a declaration rather than question from echoes of her mother's voice unfolding: "Do what you think you need to do. Know why you did it. Always know why. And at the end of the day don't regret it." The journey from "I Was" to "I Am" for KiRe is about finding her own truth. She has turned toward the acceptance of each reflection of herself in the poetic mirror from the young woman who gets straight As to the one who has not always lived authentically, as she writes, "every lie... yeah that's me too."

As the members of the Poetic Eight bring forth their naming and declarations of who they were, who they are, and who they will be, we continue to explore new beginnings and rebirth through the awakening of love. When we enter into Section Eight, love unfolds first through self-affirmation. Self-affirmation allows the adolescent girls to confront the obstacles and challenges they, and others, face with a voice of resistance. Through the awakening of love, the members of the Poetic Eight further reveal and declare what they want and what they need as they continue to uncover and maintain their voices and claim their own names and poetic identities.

Section Eight

Poetic Love

> For love alone can awaken what is divine within you.
> (O'Donohue, 1997, p. 7)

O'Donohue declares that when love awakens in your life it is a new beginning or rebirth. And as such, love is the awakening of life. It is as necessary for growth and nourishment of the soul as food is for the body. Love is the pathway to the divine and the way to one's homecoming and opening of the self toward fulfillment. It is also the process of "self-forgetting" to embrace the lives of others. While love is often sought outside of oneself, "It is at the edge of your soul" (O'Donohue, 1977, p. 8). As KiRe facilitates the poetry group session on love, she begins by describing what love is to her. In her first line she writes, "Love is everything it's not supposed to be but is…" (KiRe, in Bacon, 2009, p. 207).

In response to KiRe's poem each member begins to write what she thinks and feels about love. As the members of the Poetic Eight begin to write their thoughts and expressions of love, the room breaks into uproarious laughter and spirited exchanges. With each thought and feeling shared, they begin to build consensus on creating a collective experience of love that encompasses self-love and worth, love for family, friends and the bittersweet angst surrounding their feelings about crushes and falling in love.

> Love is caring for someone beyond all means…
> (Mishaps, in Bacon, 2009, p. 208)

> Love is heart-felt, true, sincere, honest
> (Camille, in Bacon, 2009, p. 208)

Love means commitment, trust, honesty, friendship, and feeling.
(Blue, in Bacon, 2009, p. 208)

As a dialogue ensues, there are giggles, sighs, nods, poetic snaps, and affirmation. The experience allows for more community building and unity that leads to deepen the journey as anam caras in this shared space. Voices heighten with awareness (metaphorically and literally) as each member begins to read a line that she has written until their voices blend together as one poetic sound. As the discussion continues, KiRe turns to self-love and affirmation with her inquiry, "Why is it important to love yourself before you love someone else?" I follow KiRe's lead, and after the completion of the discussion and activity, invite each member to share ways that they affirm self-love and worth, reminded of the words of O'Donohue (1997): "Sometimes it is easy to be generous outward, to give and give and give yet remain ungenerous to yourself. You lose the balance of your soul if you are a generous giver but a mean receiver. You need to be generous to yourself in order to receive the love that surrounds you" (p. 8).

Looking into the Poetic Mirror

Looking into the poetic mirror begins for the Poetic Eight by looking into the physical mirror. The writing activity is followed by an exercise in which the adolescent girls are asked to write a list of five qualities and characteristics that they love about themselves. Some of the poets, such as Mishaps and KiRe, ask if they can include more than five characteristics, which have been added. The lists that are included below provide the opportunity to find the girls' reflections in the poetic mirror.

My eyes

My lips
My personality
My thoughts/understanding
My teeth
My legs
(Lenash, in Bacon, 2009, p. 209)

My eyes (left and right)

My stomach
My attitude
My smile
My feet
My heart
My personality
My ability to write
My honesty
My self
My difference (from others)
My lips
My singing
My sarcasm
My intellect
(Mishaps, in Bacon, 2009, p. 209)

My eyes
Smile
Shyness
Photogenic(ness)
Smartness"
Maturity
(Camille, in Bacon, 2009, p. 210)

My height
My personality
My talents
My likeability
My honesty
My singing
My maturity
Sense of humor
My energy
(KiRe, in Bacon, 2009, p. 210)

The members of the Poetic Eight once again exude confidence and a positive sense of self as they rattle off the many traits and features about themselves that they love and hold dear. From size zero to size sixteen, they embrace their beauty and personalities, from sarcasm to maturity and reservation. And while I am thrilled to see adolescent girls cherish their external beauty and outward personalities, I wonder what they will find in their poetic mirrors? What can they reveal about themselves, since they have been writing in the group that resides below the surface?

The poetic mirror requires looking into the "eye" of their consciousness, internal naming, and often hidden identities. It requires once again gazing into vulnerable places (as we did in writing about death). These are the places that are not as readily revealed or accepted by others but worth embracing to experience wholeness and self-acceptance. They are the reflections of Camille's shyness that she shares in later activities, which she would like to have "fall away" to allow her to have a more audible voice; but she still holds her shyness dear in the poetic mirror.

Blue suggests that when you are experiencing self-doubt you should look in a physical mirror and declare out loud, "I love you." To look not only at your face or body, but deeply into your heart requires sight that occurs through the poetic mirror of "I Am." The space of "I Am" offers fullness and fulfillment, which are not based on society's image of beauty or peers' acceptance of who you are but on acknowledgement of your whole Being.

Seeing Self-Love

Praying the Heart by Father George A. Maloney offers that in Eastern practice there is a total integration of an individual as she meets and surrenders to the God dwelling within. This integration is said to bring about healing and fullness in order to become the "glory of God" (Maloney, 1981, p. 15). Gazing into the poetic mirror allows for this possibility by looking past physical forms to ideas and imagination. The poetic mirror opens up and reflects powerful feelings and expressions of self-love. As we enter into writing activities and discussions surrounding self-love, each girl offers her insight and poetic expression.

Mishaps writes:

> Because if you don't love yourself you can't love any one else.
> People carry traits that you carry and if you don't love your traits then how will you love theirs?
> I picked eight because my emotion is a big part of me and its not always where it should be.
> You can affirm yourself when you, " Look in the mirror and say I love you."

KiRe writes:

> It is important to love yourself before anyone else because it is impossible to have healthy, positive relationships in the future. It is also important because it isn't possible to appreciate love from someone else.
> How can you get to that stage of self love?
> Love is taught, and if it's not taught, you have to work up to it. You have to break the cycle of un-love. It is really a gift from God, to love yourself.
> God Loves You.

Camille writes:

> It is important to love yourself because it would be easier to take it from another person.

Blue writes:

> Love ur self is important because if you don't know how to love yourself then you're not going to know how to love any one else. If you don't know how to love yourself then you're not going to love anything about some one else you're going to be too busy envying them.
> You can affirm yourself by thinking of 5 things that you love about yourself. Parents (affirm in you), traits people love in you and represent you. You can get to self love when your mom and father show the importance of how much they love you and things that you do.

Collectively, the members of the Poetic Eight create a poem about the meaning and feeling of love based on a fusion of their individual ideas, voices and experiences.

> Love is a fragile pain
> Love is emotional art
> Of magic…Gotta have it!!!
> It is everything that its not supposed to be
> Love is like friendship and feelings
> It is hate, self explosion and loyalty
> Love is a heartfelt truth

> Invisible desire
> Spontaneous ride of vulnerability
> Honestly caring for someone beyond all means
> Love is sincere family
> Love is trust
> Love is joy
>
> But it SuckZ!!!
> (Poetic Eight, in Bacon, 2009, pp. 212–213)

The girls break out into "belly laughter" and give each other high fives. "Why does it suck?" I exclaim. "You know, because it has a good side but also a bad side—the pain. The reason why people cry over it." Their response is followed by more giggles and long sighs. As we move through this section, the joys and excitement of love as well as the sorrows of relationships are unfolded. This section allows for the girls to find and raise their voices in solidarity and resistance as they write to boys about what they want, will not tolerate and need to know. However, this journey begins by turning first to the voices of transition from girlhood to womanhood.

Poetry Unburdened

The lived experiences of enslaved African American women held a strong connection to struggle and freedom. The experiences of motherhood that were literally forced upon their weary bodies through brutality and rape evoked the construction in literature and writing of the outraged mother archetype. This outrage stemmed from the violent intimacy of their oppression, yet in spite of the attempts to break, subdue, and dehumanize them, they were capable still of a mother's love, passion, and dream of protecting her children from that agony. Rather than their agony defeating them, their heroism and resistance were ignited by the very abuse they, their children, and their people endured.

As the girls of the Poetic Eight transition into womanhood, they uncover the power to name who they really are with the courage and wisdom of the Black women writers who have gone before them. They unflinchingly walk through their grief, question and declare "I Am" and embrace self-love and one another. Through this process, they not only uncover their power but their wisdom and sense of knowing. As they imagine what "I Will Be," it is with their heads held high and their eyes wide open as strong Black women.

Writer and editor of *Growing Up Girl: An Anthology from Marginalized Spaces* (2006) and *Just Like a Girl* (2008), Michelle Sewell now enters this space to share her writing and lived experiences with girlhood and strong Black womanhood through her poem "Girlchild," mentioned in Section Two. Her call is similar Trish Ayers, whose poem "Dear Girl" appears in Sewell's *Just Like a Girl*.

Sewell is embraced in this space of transition from African American adolescent girl poet to Black woman writer and editor. Much like the other Black women writers who have entered this space, either in presence or through their books and published writing, she helps to navigate the wilderness from girlhood to womanhood. Sewell's experience as a poet is that many writers write because of something that they need to record. The urgency to record those experiences led Sewell to create anthologies for women and girls, and drew me to offer her anthology, *Growing Up Girl*, to my poets. Today, Sewell sounds her voice to and for the "girlchild" of the Poetic Eight, who sound back in their own voices and writing.

Like Trish Ayers in Sewell's anthology, Camille offers her own wisdom in a "Dear Girl" letter to the "GirlChild." She declares, "As a girl growing into a woman i'd say that its stressful." Camille offers her message to the "girlchild" as Sewell has done before her. Camille writes, "It seems tiring at some points, and you feel like you want to give up but you keep being persistent in it." Is it Camille's perseverance as a "girlchild" that will lead her to uncover truth, love and joy?

As Camille shares her feelings around truth, love, and joy, I am reminded again of O'Donohue's poem "Friendship Blessing" on the process of finding and becoming an anam cara. Camille offers her greatest truth as her ability to "make my parents happy." Her greatest joy, she reveals, is her family and friends. However, when asked of her greatest love, she writes, "When people make me happy" and "Talking to my best friend." She is the first adolescent girl participant in my study to openly reveal that her greatest love involves receiving (happiness) from others. I wonder how these feelings connect with other adolescent girls behind and beyond the mask. After our work in the poetry group, will these writings and feelings be deepened? Or will they possibly be changed by life circumstances and expectations of womanhood? Her unconcealing eventually leads us to her poem "IF I Were a Boy."

Divine Diva reveals, "I write poems that come from what I've experienced and what I've seen and what I go through in the process. I write poems about things and topics I think about. I might write a poem or a song or a short story. I write heavy poems, sad poems." Blue declares, "I like to write poetry and I'd like to write a book." Queen of Hearts follows, "My poetry is based more on my experiences of my friends than of me. And the way I interact with them is the way I write my poetry."

Sewell shares that as a writer you are given permission to listen to other people's lives as part of the writing, reading, or active listening process (as revealed in the poetry written for Strong Black Women in Section Four and Queen of Hearts' poetry). The process resembles the experience of not only listening to other people's stories in the group but being included in one another's lives and experiences as griottes and rhapsodes. This process leads us into the voices and stories of the "Strong and Sassy."

Voices of Strong and Sassy

> We don't talk about stuff we have a problem with until we have another problem then we bring it up. So basically everything stays the same.
> (Mishaps, in Bacon, 2009, p. 218)

As this chapter on love unfolds, the members of the Poetic Eight connect to themselves and to one another through self-love and sisterly love. These experiences and connections have been forged and created within the group over a period of time. Through their writings and responses, it continues to be revealed that friendships, romantic love, and relationships cannot endure in a space of self-denial, violence, or suffocation.

The members of the Poetic Eight also speak of another kind of suffocation that they have endured as African American adolescent girls. They speak, discuss, and write about suffocation due to pressure or jealousy from peers and conflict/tension and inner struggle. They also discuss and write with passion about challenges and issues in relationships, especially with adolescent boys and men. While violence is not a personal experience that has been inflicted upon members of the group, some of the adolescent girls have mothers, other female family members, or friends who endured being battered or otherwise abused. Both the members whose mothers or family members had been subjected to abuse, as well as those who had not, find themselves wanting to protect other girls and women, as well as guard their own hearts and bodies against these experiences.

As we unconceal self-love and resistance, the issue of adolescent girls being battered becomes a discussion and writing exercise following the physical assault on Rihanna (a well-known singer who was twenty at the time) by her boyfriend Chris Brown (also a well-known music artist and actor who was nineteen at the time). Before the "incident" was published in the school newspaper, students were asked to take a survey of their feelings about the "incident" in preparation for the article. Tragically, thirty-three percent of the high school students surveyed at Read High School report that "she deserved it." Why? How could adolescents (both boys and girls) report that a woman deserved to be battered? Did lived experiences, victim blaming, or shame keep some of the high school girls from expressing that battering was wrong? Did jealousy, pain, or denial cause other girls to say that she deserved it? I began to recall a story shared by KiRe. She and her best friend were "jumped" by girls from another school (the fight seemed to be initiated by the other girls over feelings of jealousy and territory). At that point, she began to develop feelings of distrust and animosity toward other girls (a feeling shared, initially, by some of the other girls in the group).

The patriarchal structure that has been created and enforced can be brutal to women and the cause of undo suffering and repression. This hostile environment has stifled self-affirmation, and instead, created pain and self-destruction. Reclaiming the feminine self and spirit, in this segment, begins, then, with self-affirmation for adolescent girls prior to addressing and deconstructing a violent patriarchal structure to reclaim, acknowledge, and voice the adolescent girls' strengths and embrace self-love.

I unfold the experience of pain inflicted on adolescent girls by other girls and the experience of overcoming obstacles through the lyrics of hip-hop soul singer, Mary J. Blige. Blige sings to girls and young women about rising above other people's covetousness to embrace one's own full potential. Like the Poetic Eight, Blige also unfolds the necessity of speaking truths to heal and help others heal. She offers her lyrics of self-love and healing to other girls and women in her song "Work That."

Blige's lyrics in "Work That" connect with her writing in the preface of Terrie William's 2008 book *Black Pain*. In *Black Pain,* Mary J. Blige writes how deeply moved she is by the painful stories of other African American women and men. She shares that in the faces and stories of African American women especially, she sees herself and remembers the suffering that occurred in her own life. Her lyrics in "Work That" also reveal experiences with isolation and jealousy from others who seek to keep her oppressed and ensure her failure rather than their own happiness and success. Blige is also a survivor of domestic violence. Blige's lived experiences intersect with other women who have been battered and have experienced shame surrounding the abuse (Blige, in Williams, 2008). Finally, she writes that healing occurred for her through affirming herself completely and embracing self-love and the love of God (as unfolded in section seven).

Lorde reminds us that "The true focus of revolutionary change is never merely the oppressive situations which we seek to escape, but that piece of the oppressor which is planted deep within each of us." Furthermore, she reminds us that "We sharpen self-definition by exposing the self in work and struggle together with those whom we define as different from ourselves (Lorde, 1984, p. 123).

How can the members of the Poetic Eight express their public voice and feelings about an oppressive situation? In what ways can their public voices and poetic expression further illuminate the path to eradicating the oppressor deep within each of us? Can their voices in struggle deepen their self-definition and naming?

Celebrating Strong and Sassy

Strong and Sassy

                I remember the time when she was strong and sassy...
                Born that way they say...
                Headstrong, determined, DEFIANT
"Why she switch so much?!" They'd say sucking their teeth as she'd walk by
Nobody could tell that girl nothin'. Men would holler 'em legs pretty
and long
That wouldn't stop her, oh no she'd just keep her head up and walk on by
                "Can't speak to nobody – you ain't all that!"
Them girls on the corner would laugh. They loved it when a man try and disrespect her, them girls act like they hate her – but they just jealous.
In private I even hear 'em murmur approval.
"She ain't scared of nothin' – child if I looked like that, you'd

>   see me switchin' my thang too."
>
>   Could'uv done better. Why she let that man trap her, I'll never know.
>   Beat the life out her – that's what he did.
>   The only thing she done stroll through here now, is that there baby carriage.
>   She keep that cute figure all covered up nowadays – an
>   that determination in her eye is gone. She speaks, that is when her head
>   tilt up
>   "Serve her right... thinkin' she better than us." They happy to see her spirit broke.
>   Thought she had one foot out the ghetto door... she one of us now.
>   But I remember the time she was Strong and Sassy...
>   (Bacon, in David, DuBois, & King, 1997, p. 80)

I wrote the poem "Strong and Sassy" when I was eighteen or nineteen years old. It was first published in *Returning Woman* (a literary magazine for women published by Hunter College) and then again in 1997 in *Phati'tude* (a literary magazine with a focus on writers of color). As the years have gone by, the meaning has changed for me and has come to represent the strength and fire that many of the girls I work with embody and possess. My poem has also gone on to serve as a reminder of the embodied strength and resilience that I have possessed and an understanding of the healing journey through my own intimate partner abuse that would occur later in life. From the time it was first conceived until now, "Strong and Sassy" is my poem that has received the most affirmation, identification, connection, and response by girls and women.

As I have passed it on to the members of the Poetic Eight, not only has it taken on a new meaning for me with this generation, but they have also made it their own through their responses and re-creations. I was prompted to read it to my poetry group following a discussion on learning and embracing self-love and self-worth. Many of the adolescent girls in the group had never had close (or for some any) female friends (an experience which was vastly different from my own growing up). Because some of the adolescent girls had been mistreated by other girls or women (this was not an experience or theme for all of the girls in the group but it pertains to approximately half of the members of the Poetic Eight), they (before participating in the poetry group) upheld only stereotypes of girls and women as "back stabbers" and "haters."

Based on their lived experiences, as well as the incident(s) surrounding adolescent violence and abuse, I wanted to write, read, discuss, and explore what keeps some women and girls focused on hurting one another and rejoicing in the hurt of others. What keeps some girls and women from their own true potential, success, and joy? What keeps some girls and women from reaching out to others or befriending one another? Those adolescent girls in my poetry group who previously had negative experiences with other girls and women were awestruck by their ability to bond so tightly in our poetry group. More important, I wanted to provide an opportunity for the members of the Poetic Eight to share, explore, uplift, and accept themselves in their entirety and offer support to one another. I, therefore, invited them to enter this space to claim their Strong and Sassy selves (regardless of what others might name them). By creating their own response to my poem, I encouraged them to have ownership of the words.

The Poetic Eight's Call and Responses to Strong and Sassy

Yea, I remember, with her head held high
One time a man got real close to her thigh
But she smacked it away
Turned back and said "Hey!"
With smirk on her face, she went right along
I remember saying to myself, "It won't be too long!"
I was a hater, I admit it. I wanted her to fall!
A dude was after her all the time, every day she got a call.
She was strong and so confident, I wasn't and lonely,
But now... she not the only!
(Lenash, in Bacon, 2009, pp. 224–225)

I was strong n sassy back in the days
So mature & articulate I could speak for dayz
Young, beautiful with so much prize men
Had to change and put away their pride

I was strong and sassy cute and cuddly
Fun and cool stayed in school

> I taught the teacher cuz there was nothing she could teach
> me cuz I was no fool
>
> I was strong n sassy back in the days
> Come to think about it I have yet to
> Change my ways Still strong n sassy
> You'd be amazed
> (Mishaps, in Bacon, 2009, p. 225)

Lenash and Mishaps recreate "Strong and Sassy" to reflect their poetic voices as both the embodiment of strong women and an adversary of theirs. Lenash's writings lead us through the ways in which women participate in maintaining violence: "I was a hater, I admit it. I wanted her to fall!" are acknowledgments of their own pain and unhealed emotions or shame (Richie, 1996; Williams, 2008). Through the girls' poetic calls and responses, we begin "Walking Gingerly in and around Violence."

Walking Gingerly in and Around Violence

In my poem "They Walk Gingerly," I write about women breaking the silence of domestic violence only to have their voices muted by judgment of other women who act as gatekeepers, through their explicit and implicit messages reflecting a patriarchal structure of domination and victimization.

They Walk Gingerly

> They walk gingerly around the body of the bruised.
> Then poking and prodding it with a stick, an anxiety ridden finger, a shove
>
> How did you get like this?
> What did you do?
> Neighbors inquire
>
> They want to know what brought on the onslaught of his words, the pounding of your body underneath his.
> Flattened into the wall under his supposed "restraints"
> On the bed lying lifeless

Muffled screams closed off by his hands

Had you dropped something?
Forgotten something?
Said something to make him angry?
Did you not perform your wifely duties (cooking, cleaning,
    sex...)?
Were you with another man?

No! No!
Your mind races and finally recalls an incident.
You asked for something—something he did not want to give you or
want you to have.
You asked for a cat.
Something whose warmth would keep you comforted at night.
Whose purring would lull you to sleep.
Whose body curled up by your feet at the bottom of the bed would make
you feel less fearful of him.

 But you didn't see it coming
 Him foaming at the mouth in response
 Shaking shrieking calling you names

You looked at the window and willed yourself to jump
But your feet remained planted on the ground
Your arms did not remain stationery
Flailing- they threw things in his direction
Not at him Not hitting him but as if towards him

He is on top of you now
Stuffing you like a pillow too full for its case on top of the
    mattress

The women hear your story
You shouldn't have thrown something it made him more angry
Yes, and demanding that cat, that would have given me pause
    too

> Pause? There was no pause, mute, or rewind button, just a fast forward of your mind whizzing past this violent scene
>
> Relief escapes from the listeners
> Analysis over
> Judgment drawn
>
> They rest comfy in their own lives
> Knowing safety does not evade them
>
> For they, unlike you, do not provoke their husbands
> (Bacon, in David, Bacon, & Tucker, 2011a, p. 205)

How do strong Black women recover when helping someone else not only hurts them but batters and maims their spirits? In contrast to "Strong and Sassy" and self-affirmation, I open up this segment by unfolding the perils of silencing young Black women's "Strong and Sassy" selves and the shame and suffocation that follows. I draw on scholar and activist, Beth E. Richie's study *Compelled to Crime: The Gender Entrapment of Battered Black Women* (1996). Richie's study offers a bridge from silenced voices to the dismantling of shame for African American adolescent girls (who are on the brink of strong Black womanhood) writing poetry to name themselves. Her study is based upon the experiences of primarily urban Black women who have been battered, silenced, and forced into a life of crime as a result of their societal and domestic oppression, intimate partner violence, marginalization, isolation, and encounters with a hegemonic "justice" system that further compounds their victimization based on the intersections of race and gender.

During this unfolding, I walk with caution and awareness. While some of the members of the Poetic Eight have some similarities in their childhood backgrounds and experiences, this is in no way intended to be an indication, suggestion, or implication about their futures. However, this connection is intended to illuminate the need and process for maintaining a voice, as well as active listening ears, for African American adolescent girls writing to uncover and maintain their power, as well as create a form of resistance through that writing.

From Poetic Self-Affirmation to Shame and Silence

Unlike many perceptions and stereotypes of battered Black women, Richie (1996) offers that the majority of battered Black women in her study were not abused as children (however, they did hold traditional ideas of marriage, gender roles, and identity based on their domestic ability and the patriarchal structure). Conversely, they held privileged positions within their families (often as well in school and their immediate communities) and were generally the favorite child (which sometimes led to isolation). They were rewarded for their energetic personalities, intelligence, sensitivity, charm, and/or beauty. They also reported having high self-esteem and feeling powerful as children (which created greater shame over being victimized as adults).

As children, they were seen by their families and others as positive role models and examples for other children and believed to have special gifts and talents in which other people (even outside of the family) took an interest. However, with their gifts, talents, and "exceptional status" came additional obligations and burdens, which included caring for other siblings, being the caregiver and confidante for parents, being an over-achiever in school, pleasing others, offering unwavering loyalty and attachment to their families, and feeling that they must be perfect.

Family members and others depended on them and often had unreasonable expectations of the girls' abilities and duties that the girls began to hold for themselves. These expectations and behaviors were recreated in their adult lives that frequently led them to abusive relationships in which they continued believing they were responsible for/to the abuser, for the abuse, or could change the outcome. Because of their childhood positions, they believed they could win the abuser over if they worked harder (as they did in childhood) or remained loyal. They were unable to break the silence due to shame, secrecy, and further marginalization in a hegemonic culture. Once leaving their families and communities, they were bombarded by racial disparity, inequities, exploitation and marginalization in society and the workforce.

> I can't remember when I first learned that my family expected me to work, to be able to take care of myself... It had been drilled into me that the best and only sure support was self-support. (Walker, cited in Collins, 2000, p. 183)

As girls, the battered Black women in Richie's study idealized and revered their mothers. Their mothers were respected and admired as strong women and possessed attributes such as discipline and perseverance that they sought to embody. Their relationships with their fathers were centered upon less reverence, more affection, and sympathy or pity for what they believed or perceived to be greater hardships, oppression, and limiting life circumstances that their fathers endured as Black men. They did not see girls and mothers enduring such limitations as Black women.

As adults, they often assumed the roles of their mothers as traditional, strong Black women (as unfolded in Section Four) who were "super women," endured abuse, and suffered silently in self-judgment. "How could strong, smart, pretty me get myself into this mess?" (Richie, 1996, p. 48). In some cases, the women had been told explicitly that they were to remain loyal to the abuser or feel sorry for him (a message they often received when they were children by mothers who were abused). In other cases, the message was implicit. Shame, silence, and responsibility often kept many of the battered Black women, who were once girls with high self-esteem and feelings of empowerment, trapped and voiceless when they got older.

The Power of Poetic Voices Against Violence

In Greek mythology, there is a story of two sisters, Philomela and Procne. Procne, the oldest sister, is married to Tereus, who is a wretched man. As the story unfolds, Tereus is to retrieve Philomela for a visit. Upon seeing her, he "falls in love." Much like the batterers revealed in this segment, Tereus's feelings are described as love; however, his emotions are actually centered on lust and his actions violent and deceptive.

Tereus tells Philomela that her sister has died and forces her into a relationship with him (the implication is that he rapes her). Once she learns that her sister is still living, she threatens to tell her and expose him to the community. Tereus fears her speaking the truth and in a rage cuts out her tongue and locks her away. However, Philomela manages to get a message to her sister, who comes to free her.

Procne, out of revenge and punishment for what Tereus has done to her sister, murders their son. As the sisters flee from Tereus, who is on the verge of killing them, the gods turn them into birds so they can escape. Philomela becomes a swallow. Swallows can twitter but cannot sing, much like Philomela because her tongue has been cut out. The gods turn Procne into a nightingale because of her deep sadness over murdering her son. The nightingale's song is the sweetest because it is brought forth through sorrow (Hamilton, 1969).

As I recall this story, what stands out most to me is the power of women's voices. So feared were their voices, that Tereus cut out Philomela's tongue rather than allow her to speak the truth. And while Philomela is never able to speak again, her connection to her sister and her sister's voice permits her to once again be free.

In this section, the members of the Poetic Eight express their voices on behalf of themselves and their "sisters." Through their poetry writing, they speak directly to oppression to be heard by one another and to be free. As Blue's voice is sounded in her letter "Dear Scrub" in solidarity with girls that are battered, I hear the echoes of Levin's revelation. "I can hear myself when I listen to the other."

> I can hear myself when I listen to the other: I
> can hear myself in the other, or in the position
> of the other… I can hear the other when I listen to myself…
> (Levin, 1989, p. 182)

Levin describes the experience of listening, hearing, connecting with our selves, voices, and positions of others, which allow our role identifications to become blended, changed, or even reversed. With this expression and exploration, a sense of resistance and voice of social justice are created. As we unconceal violence against adolescent girls and women in our poetry group, the members of the Poetic Eight share their voices and denounce the suffocating experiences of shame and degradation of violence. Blue brings out her voice of justice and direction as she writes to men who hit women in the following letter:

> Dear Scrub,
> 2 the boy that hit my sistah understand this does not make you more of a man. Matter of fact you're not a man at all. And if you think you are then you have been miseducated…
> I know your mother taught you better then that. Think about how your mother would feel being beat… How can we trust you boys? Think about the younger ones you are influencing with this bad behavior. Also think about the generation of unborn baby boy[s] who would later be in your shoes. Be a man for others who can't and don't try to be a man. Please Listen [about] not being a man who beats his wife, girlfriend, or friend…

So when you ever start to think about hitting or laying a hand on a girl or woman. Think about my sistahz and your sistahz too. (Blue, in Bacon, 2009, p. 233)

Blue's letter responds to her later request that boys sit down with girls to listen with openness to what girls and women have to say. She seeks to share the point of view of and for girls and women who have been in abusive relationships or have been witness to such relationships. During another poetry group "check-in," Queen of Hearts shares that in class a boy was pulled off of a girl that he was attempting to batter. Mishaps enters the conversation with her own story of being grabbed by a boy who was sitting at a desk behind her, attempting to fondle her. After a lengthy discussion, we decide to create poetry and writings around the incidents that occurred that day and other similar incidents and events that had occurred in their lives, the lives of their loved ones, and in society.

I ask each member to think of what they would like to write to the boys and men in each of the incidents or to boys and men in general who batter, humiliate, or otherwise attempt to degrade them or other women and girls in any way (physically, sexually, emotionally, verbally, and psychically). In response, Queen of Hearts declares, "I would like to read a letter to those who harm women. I would like to read that to them. Because once they hear it [it could be like] 'damn I never looked at it that way.' I would love for them to catch on to that." After writing her poem, Queen of Hearts, declares, "I actually let my anger go. Writing [helps me] lose my anger."

Queen of Hearts writes in solidarity with women and girls who have been battered. However, she seems to make a distinction between girls who are battered and are victims and those who are not. Is the difference for Queen of Hearts based on who cries and who defends herself in naming themselves battered and in need of protection and voice? As we have unfolded self-love and naming of strong Back women, is it possible to recognize that a strong Black woman, who is not "weak or harmless," can be battered? Queen of Hearts' unfolding also seems to chronicle the voices and responses to "Strong and Sassy" as she writes of a woman whose spirit becomes broken in an abusive relationship. Queen of Hearts, much like Blue and the sisters in the tale of Philomela, writes of the power of women offering their voices for one another to be free.

Mishaps shares,

> Basically, it's like you can't escape. As a female, we walk around and have guys calling us out of our names. You can't escape that. A guy is not going to change overnight and we have to suffer for it as females. And if he's raised around people who teach him how to do that, we have to suffer for it. Older men teach young people. I think that older men need to take control. Fathers teach younger men. Stop saying certain things to teach their kids how to disrespect females.

"And I think," Blue interjects, "they [the boys] should also sit down with us and listen to what we have to say and how we feel about them doing certain stuff that we disapprove of, and they will get our point of view." How do we create a space where girls can feel safe and share their fears? How, as Blue states, do we sit young men down to have them listen to the once-silenced voices of African American adolescent girls and women? As this section continues, this dialogue begins by inviting the voices of male allies to walk gingerly in this space (Bacon, 2009, p. 236).

In KiRe's unfolding, she invites her potential boyfriend to step from behind the mask with her, "…to show me the person you really are." She expresses through her writing that she is not looking for a fairy tale, "I want you to be real." The members of the Poetic Eight, unfold self-love and affirmation as the means to a healthy relationship with themselves and with others; KiRe's writing reveals the need for the same level of introspection from boys, "I want you to tell me exactly what you need."

The Poetic Eight girls share their voices and feelings on justice and love as they tell boys and men how they really feel, what they don't like, and what hurts them with power, fire, and truth. As they discuss and write their lived experiences and the previous experiences of others, they do not have to wait for another problem or hurt to occur before they can "bring it up" to "finally" get to the point of healing, love of and by another. As they share their strengths and truths, the members of Poetic Eight allow their needs and vulnerability (once again undergoing change and releasing burdens) to be known as well.

Yet, as this segment comes to a close, questions begin to arise for me. If the Poetic Eight were a group of boys, would their needs and writings be perceived the same way? Would they feel an urgency to explain and justify their feelings and writings? What are the expectations of adolescent girl and women writers in contrast to those of adolescent boys and men?

I have been asked by some men (in and out of education, writing, and the realm of academia) if it is necessary to harp on "these things," or if this is really about male bashing? I also have seen men squirm with discomfort when hegemony, violence, abuse, or pain are discussed by women, especially young women and adolescent girls. The adolescent girl poets in my study have been asked by some males, "Don't you write anything happy? "There seems to be a theme here." They have responded, "We write reality" (ours or others), or "It's easier to write the happy poems once you can write out the challenges or the pain," and "a lot of people like to shy away from the hard stuff." However, the girls of the Poetic Eight—along with Keisha and many of the other adolescent girls and young women I have taught, worked with, and learned from—do not shy away from the "hard stuff;" rather, they have chosen to call it out and write their way through it instead.

Poetic Change: Gendered Complexities

Once discussions deepen with candid conversation, honesty, real emotion, and sensitivity, what often follows for male educators, poets/writers, and/or fathers (who previously felt or expressed discomfort or even outright denial) is the question of what they can possibly do to support the process (of empowerment, expression and identity naming) for African American adolescent girls. They also question: Do men begin to uphold Black feminism? To this, I often have responded by sharing the ways in which men can enter into dialogue and discussion with girls and women, and even enter into the space themselves as Black feminists. The process of entering this space begins with the acknowledgment that a problem does exist in the current patriarchal structure, followed by actively listening to the stories and voices of the girls and women who unfold their experiences (Bacon, 2009).

Entering into this space for the purpose of authentic discussion is crucial for Being to occur behind the mask. Men must come into this space with an understanding of the need sometimes for silence and with questions rather than expectations, assumptions, and ready-made answers to experiences that they have not yet heard or encountered. As I explore this space of gendered complexities, I unfold questions, expectations, and assumptions of girlhood and boyhood.

I now reflect on my own girlhood. I had a diverse group of playmates consisting of Nigerian, Swedish, African American, Italian American, Jamaican American, Irish American, Jewish, Protestant and Catholic boys and girls. Many of my playmates were from traditional families, and I considered my family to be more progressive than theirs. My parents did not practice or enforce traditionally defined gender roles in our household. And unlike many of the other mothers, my mother worked outside of the home and had a career.

My two close neighbor friends, Natalie" and "Janine," were from traditional Italian American households. We would play together after school, along with our sisters or the neighborhood boys "Maurice," "Mike," and "Cheidu" or "Harry." When we played with the boys, we would have water fights, dodge ball games, or snowball fights—basically anything that required a moving target. Mostly, we girls were the target for the boys. We would shriek, squeal and run for cover.

Yet balls and snow were not the favorite weapon of choice. Rather, the favorite weapon was picked from Maurice's parents Dogwood tree. Each one of us would take turns climbing the tall tree, past the delicate pink flowers to the bright, hard, red berries. Once we climbed back down, the berries would be hurled with impressive force at the faces of the opposite sex. The boys always took this game rather seriously and would throw the berries with much more fervor, causing greater damage to our bodies. They also seemed to derive pleasure from causing pain and making us cry—especially if that crying sent us running home.

Many a day Natalie, Janine, and I would run shrieking home covered in hives or with swollen eyes from repeatedly being hit in the face by the berries. In the midst of an attack, we would retreat. Sometimes we would retreat crying and at other times muttering furiously, but we always returned to the "game." We relied on our verbal prowess and sage tongues to issue a stern lecture, temporarily persuasive argument on the dangers of violence, or enlightened counsel and ministry to the "lost souls" also known as "the boys."

These "sessions" often involved hands on unformed hips and fingers wagging in the air. On gentler days, they involved soothing tones, compassion for the boys' stories of having their intentions misunderstood, motherly advice, and forgiveness. We believed that our pearls of wisdom and sincerity would inspire them to rise to higher emotional ground or at, the very least, stop smashing our little faces with hard berries. But in reality, it never did.

And while we were all "nice" and "good" kids playing a relatively innocent game that was not designed to inflict any real pain or injury, it still seems to unfold a deeper meaning and indication of traditional gender roles, expectations, and interactions (Bigner, 1994). The day that stands out most in my mind is the one when I ran into the kitchen to grab ice for the eye that was quickly beginning to close shut. Fighting back anger and tears, I was going to nurse my wounds and quickly run back outside to my neighbor's house again. Before I could leave, my mother stopped me to ask me what happened. I rapidly rattled off a list of occurrences without so much as taking a breath. My mother looking shocked, then asked either "Why are you going back there?" or "Why do you keep going back there?" And while the reasoning of a nine- or ten-year-old is undoubtedly much less complicated than that of a grown woman, sometimes the concept or thought process can be similar. It never occurred to me not to go back. Frankly, I did not know there was an alternative. It simply seemed to be what girls did—endure pain or suffering and what boys did—inflict pain or suffering. And while these experiences are painful, sharing them for the purpose of emancipation is *The Truth That Never Hurts* (Smith, 1998).

I unfold this story and the ethnic and racial diversity of my playmates for two primary reasons. The first is to elucidate the effect of sexism on African American girls and women. Black feminist writer Barbara Smith states that this simple statement is "rhetoric to the contrary" (Smith, 1998, p. 41). Therefore, I seek to acknowledge intersectionality and racial and gender oppression of African American women and girls in my story and in my study. The second is to acknowledge that the aggressive behavior of some boys (which society generally depicts as behaviors displayed by African American boys) is often overlooked when displayed by European American/White boys (Crenshaw, 2016; Kunjufu, n.d.; Love, 2019). However, this study is focused on the lived experience of African American adolescent girls.

I recognize that there are many gender stereotypes that are displayed in my story. Furthermore, I acknowledge that there are many girls and boys who do not have such stereotypical experiences. I am also mindful of making broad and sweeping generalizations about gender or sex based on a specific recollection.

Yet, as an educator who has worked with students from pre-kindergarten to graduate school, I see a similar dynamic year after year. As in my own childhood experience, I see girls and young women of all ethnicities, religions, cultural backgrounds, socio-economic statuses, and "race," nurturing, counseling, yelling, condoning, excusing, lecturing, blaming themselves, blaming other girls and women, cajoling, explaining, crying, and begging boys and young men to stop hurting them or to change their patterns of behavior.

I've also noticed a shift in the behavior of some girls who now attempt to imitate the boys' expressions and even batter them back (as unfolded in Queen of Hearts' poem). But often what I still do not see is girls and young women being given or giving themselves the permission to acknowledge that they do not have to endure or deserve being pelted by berries (as a metaphor for suffering or violence). I also do not often see boys being given or giving themselves permission to opt out of stereotypical male roles and behavior, even if it means being the male outsider on the playground.

As I explore the needs of African American adolescent girls based on their poetry and reflections, I connect with the work of Gary Lemons (2008). Lemons explores his position as an outsider on the metaphorical male playground in his book *Black Male Outsider*. Furthermore, I invite male ally, poet, feminist, and educator Omari Daniel through his work and writings on "I Am Not a Man" to enter this space with the Poetic Eight as a guest speaker and active listener (Bacon, 2009).

Black Male Outsider

Gary Lemons (2008) writes in *Black Male Outsider* the ways in which he, as a professor, has used the study and teaching of Black feminism through Black feminists' writings and autobiography. He shares that they not only transformed his professional and personal life but saved them both by allowing him to fuel his passion, connect more deeply with his students, embrace social activism, dismantle racism and sexism, redefine himself and others, and move his students toward self-empowerment and inner healing. In addition to my own dialogues and discussions around these topics, I have chosen to invite former English co-teacher, friend, and writer Dr. Omari Daniel into this poetic space. He enters as an African American male, high school teacher, poet, academic, ally, feminist, and father. Daniel shares his lived experiences, writings, and reflections on manhood, which have provided him with deeper understanding and communication with African American adolescent girl students. He offers his story, writings, and reflections with the members of the Poetic Eight. But, more important, he offers his "listening ears" as a poetic male ally to hear their stories and their voices.

A fundamental goal of male feminism or male feminists is for men to "unlearn" traditional patriarchal systems that support and encourage oppression and marginalization (in terms of gender, race, ethnicity, class, and sexual orientation). Essentially, men "unlearn" manhood as it has been created as a "performance," caricature and mask (Lemons, 2008, p. xviii). It is also critical to acknowledge gender expansive roles and identities in my work, which includes non-binary and transgender identities.

Furthermore, in Black feminism it is acknowledged that one form of marginalization, such as racism, cannot be dismantled while maintaining or upholding another form of oppression and marginalization, such as sexism (or vice versa). Barbara Smith (1998) writes about the dismantling of race and gender oppression in *The Truth That Never Hurts* and exposes the necessity of eradicating such contradictions for the emancipation of women and men (humans).

These same truths spill over onto the pages throughout the section on love as the members of the Poetic Eight offer their poetry to men who batter women as they redefine what they have experienced, observed, or previously described as "love." As I continue to unfold these writings, guest speaker/poet Daniel is now invited to walk gingerly with us. But first, he must acknowledge that a problem in the structure does exist and offer his naming not only as an ally but as "Not a Man." Daniel offers his naming by acknowledging the names, qualities, and characteristics the adolescent girls, through their experiences, or the experiences of their loved ones, have come to know as "me."

I Am Not a Man

I am six foot three, can bench press 435 lbs, fathered two children, look better than Taye Diggs, but apparently, I am not a man. This fact has been delivered to me by waves of female students washing into my classroom during planning periods or lunch. Their words have washed up onto my conscious and eroded my definition of who I thought I was. I thought I was a man. In fact, I thought I was "the man." However, I was wrong, wrong, wrong and I have never been prouder to be wrong in my life. I am glad I am not a man.

"Dr. Daniel. I need to talk to you." This phrase has become part of my daily life as a teacher. Unless I am in class, I know I need to focus my attention on the brave eyes now trying to fight back inevitable tears. Another fragile young woman has made a choice to seek me out. I am humbled by this choice every single time. They did not choose their fathers, grandfathers, uncles, best friends, boyfriends, brothers, counselors, or psychiatrists. They choose me. I was honored to be viewed as "the choice" but I could not help but wonder why? Why did a girl whose man told her to abort her baby because she was not his idea of a real woman tell me "When he said that, most girls would have cried 'oh Daddy,' or 'oh best friend' or 'oh So and So,' but she cried 'oh Mr. Daniel.'" Why did she want me? What kind of person am I?

I know I am not quite as sane as other teachers. I know I like to play around some and teach simultaneously. I also know that students know I will tell them the truth no matter how painful it is to hear. I am pretty sure my students trust me and know I am not here to judge them. They also know I am all about them improving their lives and developing their own identities, voices, confidence, and love of self so that they can conquer our cruel world. But a lot of teachers are like that right? This did not explain why so many girls were telling me things that only their diaries knew. Was I a living diary?

The issues that they have brought to me are overwhelmingly sensitive. I don't even know how to begin to express them. I guess I will try the band-aid method and just rip them right off. Maybe then I can get through the list without crying with and for my girls again. Rapes, molestations, loss of virginity, asking me if they should lose their virginity, believing they were ugly, that their bodies were ugly, believing a boy who said, "I love you," believing they are not important, wondering how to survive being labeled a ho, how to survive a father believing you are a female dog, believing you should not be alive any longer, believing..... I can't make it. There are just too many wounds. There simply is no pill to dull this pain. It would essentially be taking aspirin for a bullet to the heart. I never learned the lesson that men can't cry or feel.

Why were they telling me these things? That question has haunted me these last few years, until I was blessed with an answer last week. A young lady told me "I hate boys. I hate men. I do not trust them. I ignore them all at home and in school. I would never tell a man anything about myself. They are all dogs and disgusting." Then she proceeded to tell me something devastating. I asked her "If you hate men so much, then why are you telling me? You do realize I am a man?" Her answer struck my soul like lightening. No, you are not. You are not a man, you are different."

I saw the light. For an infinite number of girls today, the term man has come to represent darkness, fear, manipulation, hatred, depression, or pain. For an infinite number of girls today, a man has turned into a sexual predator, a liar, an abusive mate, a thief, a pervert, a foe, a taker, a user, a dragon breathing pure evil itself.

I was not doing anything special; I was simply not doing anything terrible. I was no monster—I mean man. I was different because I had no ulterior motives when I talked to them. I was strange because I wanted what was best for them. I was weird because I told them I loved them and meant it. I was an odd creature because I helped them to understand they had the power to heal themselves, and to love themselves despite the "perceived flaws" and unfortunate circumstances. I was not a man because men don't do those things for women. A man can't just be an honest, open, caring friend to a woman, therefore in their books, I was not a man. I was safe.

Not being a man is a gift and a curse. The gift is that I get to be there for a girl when they feel no one else is there. It is the ultimate gift, simple, yet eloquent; it is the chance to help. By not being a man, I get to matter.

The curse is not being depressed or burdened by so much sadness. I will listen to them all day if I have to because they need help slaying the beasts in their lives. The curse is having to prove myself to every girl I teach, year after year, that I am not a man. The curse is because of my genetics, many girls in need will not think to talk to me in fear that I am just a man. I am cursed because I have to go home to talk to my two sons. At the innocent ages of three and five. I wish I could just have the talk about them growing up to be anything they want in life. Instead, because of you (and honestly the man I was in college) I must tell them they can grow up to be anything but men. Thanks man.
(Daniel, in Bacon, 2009, p. 250)

After Daniel's reading, Blue inquires, "What do you mean when you say you're happy not being called a man?" In response, Daniel offers his feelings candidly about the pressure to prove your manhood and "act hard" and not show your soft side. "You realize at some point that you are not allowed to be a human being anymore. You are not allowed to be vulnerable. So, trying to play up to that [acting hard] or buy in to it… becomes a sad existence for you as a man. [It's] a dead end." It is through Daniel's process as a writer and pro-feminist, living behind the mask, that he is able to reach his inner self and enter this space to be heard and received by its members.

As this section unfolds self-love and writing as a tool for justice and resistance, I connect with Daniel's words as he shares with the Poetic Eight. "When I first started writing I was making up stuff and it was terrible. Eventually I started writing about my life." He tells the girls with his voice unwavering, "Your first weapon is your pen. You've got a tool to beat this world." What tool or weapon will they use as Dr. Daniel facilitates the group today? Will they write from their hearts, as they do with me, or "put up a front?"

I remember the words of KiRe from a previous one-on-one discussion with me: "Guys just bring a different vibe. And a lot of girls put up a front when guys are around. Maybe it's just woman's nature. To be the best one. The attitude would have been different and the outcome of the club would have been different [if boys participated]" (KiRe, in Bacon, 2009, p. 253).

Yet, as Daniel unconceals himself and listens actively to the Poetic Eight's voices, their questions, reflections, and lived experiences begin to flow from behind the mask.

Camille writes during our next meeting how she felt about Dr. Daniel revealing "I Am Not a Man."

> I really liked this poem because it's something I would want a man to be. Someone I could talk to about anything and get good feedback on it. In this poem this is a person you could tell secrets to. Thoughts, feelings anything you want and accepted the conversation with no rejection. Women can talk to him as if he were another woman when physically you saw he was a man. He was a person who helped you understand completely yourself and the situation. (Camille, in Bacon, 2009, p. 253)

> I felt the weight come off my chest because the words that was brought to my head what a man is was said in the poem. The poem made me speechless because that is how I feel about boys/men I would tell you what a man is and can easily tell you what I think a man is. But I won't know what a real man is or a boy until I come in contact with a real man. The poem also made me understand from a man perspective what a real man is or should be. (Blue, in Bacon, 2009, p. 254)

Camille and Blue uncover the power to name what a man is based on their discoveries of what a man is not. As they travel through their questions of "If I Were a Boy?" to their experiences with "I Am Not a

Man" they arrive at a place of homesteading by remembering their own names.

Remembering Your Name

Blue's voice follows, "[There are] a lot of things that go on in a girl's life especially inside which can create conflict outside which is a reflection of what's going on in the inside. Being hurt by a peer, a loved one or just a friend. Losing self-esteem."

Blue explores the experience of girls and women who lose the power to speak their own names in her poem "Positive." In "Positive," Blue writes about a woman who contracts HIV as she struggles to find love through sex and "That feeling of sexual healing." Blue's poem takes us through the disconnection between emotions and bodily sensations that drive the woman in her poem to forget her identity/naming to get "lost in his name" (White, 1995).

Positive

> She says his name, forgetting her own
> Bodies clingin, a lustful woman singin
> The words in her heart
> And ooww, while this woman sings
> She gets lost in his name
> While forgetting that his aint the same as yesterday's
> Today it's Pete, the one that massages her feet
> While yesterday was Sam, who made her body go "Damn!"
>
> And while she whispers "Pete...Pete"
> She is still remembering Sam... but only because he made her body go "Damn!" and Pete aint doin all the things he could
> or that she wish he would so that she can get that feeling.
> That feeling of sexual healing...
>
> And though Pete aint all that good, she know he would do it [if] he
> Could, but he can't, so she goes back to Sam...
> See Sam knows her body real well, so his name is what she yells.
> Taking her body around and around, while deeper and deeper
> He goes down.

> She thinks to herself "Oh, hell yes!" This man Sam is definitely the best!"
>
> Now while he doesn't "like" to use condoms
> She just thinks "Well, what the hell!"
> Forgetting 1,051,875 people die a year from those words.
> And as she's yelling his name, she forgets it won't be the same
> Because afterwards, she senses it to be all wrong.
> Still the hormones are pulling her along to her grave.
>
> She takes a pregnancy test to see if her body can progress, but
> It's positive... but so is she in the case of HIV AIDS, now
> Aint that some bullshit!
>
> She should have said that when he said "They take away the fun, baby." Little did she know, they could have saved her life, but
> Now she gotta try to fight, her fears, her fam, her friends, and disease.
> But she aint have to be here, standing all alone, just
>
> Because while saying his name, she forgot her own.
> (Blue, in Bacon, 2009, pp. 255–256)

What does it mean to forget your name to say another name? How do adolescent girls remember their own names not to be left "standing all alone" and forgotten? As the section has unfolded on self-love, love of another, the voice of resistance and allies, I reconnect the writings of the Poetic Eight with the words of Daniel behind the mask.

> Think about the number of people in your life who know exactly who you are. Who know the inner you. When that person says they love you. How do you know they are saying the truth? Good, bad, sad. And they are not going anywhere. Fast forward to the men you know. To love you means they have to know you. So how can someone say that they love you without knowing the inner you.
> (Daniel, in Bacon, 2009, p. 256)

As I reflect on the meaning of adolescent girls and women losing and remembering their names, I now offer my poem, "He Carries in His

Heart" to these writings on self-love and naming. "Do not throw your pearls to pigs..." is shared in Matthew, 7:6 in the Holy Bible (1984). "My pearls" in my poem represent not only wisdom or knowing but a sense of self-worth, self-esteem, and identity that are expressed through naming. In my poem, it is the truth and path of personal identity and fulfillment of dreams that lead to emancipation. "He Carries in His Heart" is written about remembering the name that was forgotten to remember his—your own.

> He carries in his heart my tears
>   imprinted like footprints
>   walking through the consciousness of his mind.
>   He holds images of me closer and closer still
>   thinking if he shuts his eyes and squinches his face
>   i cannot break free
> from the grasp that binds us as forcefully as his remembrances
>   He does not see that I have vanished many years
>   before
>   as I have grown older and gone to cast my pearls
>   at the feet of my own dreams.
> He carries the pictures of the past with the breath of
>   "remember when?"
>   I do remember... which is why I leave him
> (Bacon, 2009, pp. 256–257)

I am reminded of poetry writing in *Catch the Fire: A Cross-Generational Anthology of Contemporary African-American Poetry* (Gilbert, 1998). Poet Asha Bandele—a survivor of depression, domestic violence, self-abuse. and racism—writes to a woman who has taken her life to end her similar suffering. Bandele offers living words and a name to the woman in her poem "The Subtle Art of Breathing." In the poems that I have shared in this segment, Blue has written "Positive," and I have unfolded "He Carries in His Heart" for other adolescent girls and women who have also forgotten their names.

Bandele writes, "I'm gonna be even more than a survivor I'll be a celebrant inside myself..." She invites the woman, in her imagination, to join her in remembering her own name by becoming "your own sensual dance partner in high-heeled shoes fine as hell girl & so so so fulla life" (Bandele, in Gilbert, 1998, p. 35).

Whether the adolescent poets received unconditional support and love, or relationships were healed or reconciled with boys, men, peers, parents, or other loved ones in their lives, members of the Poetic Eight eventually made the decision to take the chance to be heard and be "so fulla life." They also risked being vulnerable by sharing and writing their stories and the stories of others. Revelation, truth, and passion carry us into the next section on divinity. Spirituality and divinity are themes that the members of the Poetic Eight often reveal through their discussions and writings, both of which give them the strength to move toward Being and love. According to metaphysician William Warch, "If you need love, you draw it from absolute love, God" (1977, p. 4). Divinity, in Section Seven, is expressed through the Poetic Eight's and my relationship and writings surrounding God, religion, or spirituality, finding the anam cara within and without, and a final path to homesteading.

Section Nine

Honoring the Divine

Hermes, in Greek mythology, was not only a messenger between gods and mortals but a messenger between the living and the dead (Steiner, 1989). Embracing our divinity offers us the space to be as Hermes in such a communion. For Blue and Mishaps, their messages have been delivered from their thoughts and remembrances to their deceased mothers. And as pain is transformed and joy is revealed, a relationship with the anam cara is forged. Throughout this poetic unfolding, the girls in the Poetic Eight connect to one another through their shared experiences of suffering, friendship. and joy that lead them to the path of anam cara. It is through the relationship with an anam cara that recognition and belonging are uncovered and the "hidden intimacies" of the writer's life are revealed (O'Donohue, 1997, p. xviii). The friendships that are born in this sacred space of one's heart and remembrances of the past open the way for friendships of the soul (Bacon, 2009).

In this individual and collective journey, we are each called upon to honor and protect our memories and lived experiences, as well as those of one another as we are upheld "Safe in the Heart of Another" (Hollingsworth, as cited in White-Hood, 1989, p. iv). And with this safety, homecoming and homesteading are blessed with the unfolding of true friendship. This journey with the anam cara further leads us to God (in many names) "as the divine anam cara" (O'Donohue, 1997, p. 132).

Poetic Faith

Walsch (1995, 1997) shares in *Conversations with God* that our lives are an expression of creation rather than discovery. Creation must include a sense of knowing that represents absolute faith. Faith is often known Biblically as "being sure of what we hope for and certain of what we do not see" (Hebrews, 11:1). Moving into an active sense of knowing and believing often requires intuition, trust, and higher consciousness to connect and experience a "belief in what you cannot see or prove or touch" (Gilbert, 2006, p. 175). It is faith, knowing, and creation that reveal clarity. It is also faith and self-love that eventually allow the members of the Poetic Eight to experience "I Was," "I Am" and "I Will Be" holistically. According to Heidegger (1969), in metaphysics there is thought and a presence of wholeness that allow for the recognition of difference and variation, while integrating diverse parts into a whole.

> Individuality is the I Am...
> (Warch, 1977, p. 23)

In integrating diverse poetic parts into a whole, phenomenologist and writer George Steiner (1989) shares that God's presence is possible through experiences, exploration, and the meaning of artistic creation. Through meaningfulness, a path is created to the formation of living words. According to Steiner, words do not create God; rather, God creates life through words.

Although phenomenology and poetry are grounded in metaphysics and the divine, I do not introduce God or spirituality into the classroom, not even as a poet or phenomenological researcher. Also, I do not initiate discussions around these topics as my research is primarily guided by the lived experiences of my participants. Therefore, I am struck by the fact that when the adolescent girl poets are asked to pick any topic or theme that they want to write about or facilitate, many of their selections center around God and the principles of divinity.

Poetic Principles

In my study, the opening of this poetic space follows the acknowledgment of sorrow and grief that once kept members of the Poetic Eight isolated. Uncovering truth, joy, and love led us to the final journey of homesteading. In this space of homesteading, I ask each poet to name her greatest truth, joy, and love. Furthermore, I reenter this space as a co-participant to realize my own truth and joy.

Mishaps writes that her greatest truth is that "love conquers all" and "everyone has a sensitive side." Having been exposed to violence and pain, her revelation and acceptance of sensitivity seem to create another passage from the wilderness to homesteading, which is a place that allows for vulnerability and self-acceptance. When Mishaps speaks and writes of her greatest joy, she first scribbles on the page that her greatest joy is "my sisters" and "when they are happy." She then scratches through her writings, and instead changes the latter phrase to "When I'm doing right by God" (Mishaps, in Bacon, 2009, p. 262).

I wonder what the shift means for her. What is the power in her naming of her joy as an older sister who is also their surrogate mother? Does scribbling through her sisters' joy to her own quest of "doing right by God" reveal an even greater connection to the universal? Mishaps has just begun to discover feelings of wanting to be protected rather than always assuming the role of the protector. Where will these feelings lead her now that our poetic work together is almost complete?

I am drawn to remembering the discussions and reflections of Mishaps, Divine Diva, and Blue, who recall the lived experiences of their journeys as their mothers' children and their own experiences with relationships. I am drawn, in particular, to Mishaps' experience in her witnessing of "love" that is abusive and destructive. I also journey in the darkness to recollect my own writings and experiences of such relationships and the rewriting of those experiences to offer support and guidance for other young women as well as my own healing.

Praise Poetry

Blue originally introduces the topic of God and spirituality to the poetry group. However, when she selects the topic for facilitation, she changes the topic and discussion to God and religion, which become prominent themes in and for the group. "My mom was so religious, and when I make poetry about God it touches me... I feel God is my strength, my higher purpose, my higher thought. When I touch on something religious, it [her feelings and her poetry] comes pouring out..." And with her unfolding, she seems to develop a new style of poetry—praise poetry.

Why I Praise

I pray to you for wisdom
I pray to you for strength
His eye is on the sparrow

My love will never narrow
For God is my hero, more
Then that but a creation for

Which I walk upon
Blessing me with charm of life
With heaven of holy light

That shines through the sun light
Love the feeling of praising you
Calling upon God when my nights are blue

My soul belongs to you
If only they can see
What we hold underneath

Is a master piece
Of his work, so don't give up
God knows time is rough

And when you had enough
But like it says he won't give
You more than you can bare

God expresses his love for you
In difference and hardships…So I

Sing because I'm free
God installs all my hopes and dreams
Look at me giving praise for every little thing

Read between the lines God
Is my only prize, my rhyme
G.O.D. is the song I sing inside
So when I say I'm blessed

Nothing can compare to this blessing
(Blue, in Bacon, 2009, p. 264)

Praise poetry allows Blue to offer gratitude or praise for her life and the love she believes God expresses, even during her hardships and grief. After her mother's death, she finds a connection to her mother spiritually and the ways in which she feels that she is "blessed" in life even in the little things. "Look at me giving praise for every little thing." Much like Freire (2000) and Walker (1997), Blue embraces freedom from her pain through her mind, inner thoughts, and beliefs while working to change her life circumstances. Embracing divine love and freedom allows Blue to create and maintain her hopes and dreams.

Blue connects with her deceased mother through religion and faith, while Queen of Hearts connects with her feelings of being forsaken by her father through her faith. In her writing, Queen of Hearts experiences her abandonment by her father as being forsaken by God. However, as her father reconnects with her, the meaning of being forsaken is transformed. Through the reconnection with her father, she expresses gratitude for what he has forsaken. "I thank you for keeping me in your thoughts, and all you have forsaken me for."

Finding Meaning in the Divine

While praise, worship, spirituality, and faith differ within the group, spirituality still appears to be one of the greatest pulls and strengths (along with writing, shedding tears, and music) for overcoming grief and embracing joy for members of the group.

> ...As you pull me up
> From the dark place...
> (Queen of Hearts, in Bacon, 2009, p. 267)

The Poetic Eight uncover their power to name themselves and heal their relationships through their faith, love, and God's "holy embrace." While the Poetic Eight's lived experiences vary, they feel united in the power of the divine that "Keeps me alive." As I unfold this section, I must acknowledge that there are many practices, beliefs, and faiths that have not been included. In this chapter, as in this phenomenological study, I have been led by the voices and expressions of my participants.

Honoring the Divine Everywhere

As I return to hermeneutics and metaphysics, I note that Heidegger (1969) describes metaphysics as "a statement about God, because the deity enters into philosophy" (p. 55). Heidegger further acknowledges as he speaks of philosophy that the deity enters everywhere and brings us toward Being as "always and everywhere" (p. 61). Heidegger (1993) defines metaphysics as the "Interpretation of beings and the forgetfulness of Being..." (p. 91). The metaphysical is revealed in these poetic unfoldings as we embrace Dasein. Heidegger reveals Dasein as states of emotion such as joy, excitement, or anxiety. Heidegger travels through anxiety, much as the Poetic Eight, to realize that it is this state that forces one to face life, death, and Being (1993).

Life, death, and Being have been represented through the poetry of the Poetic Eight. Poets have been described as people or groups who intuitively offer deep understanding of the human experience with an accuracy that is delicate and a perception that is empathetic. In terms of divinity, poets have been said to raise consciousness and act as visionaries (Woodward, 1987). How do poets act as visionaries but not get entangled or attached to their visions? As I open the final section and contemplate the meaning of the pedagogy of poetry, I begin by honoring the visions of poets (Bacon, 2009).

I end Section Nine on divinity and open Section Ten on the pedagogy of poetry with the invitation for phenomenologists, "other mothers and fathers," culturally responsive educators, spiritualists, activists, community members, writers/poets, human scientists, humanitarians, and human beings (along with the many other names we call ourselves in this field and beyond) to learn and teach from the heart. I charge poets and educators to embrace the love of learning and inquiry, open our hearts and minds to creativity, and honor the inner beauty of each student poet. If we guard the thoughts and imaginings of every student as if she were a budding poet, as well as guard our own dreams, power may not only be uncovered, but it may be maintained.

Section Ten

The Pedagogy of Poetry

According to the Webster Dictionary, home is a place where someone lives. It is also a dwelling place, like the poetry space, together with, as family, or a social unit. Home is an environment that offers security and happiness or a place of refuge. Home can also be where something was originated, or someone was born, or has lived for a long period (which in the poetry space can be a physical place, emotion, or heart of another, like the heart of a mother). And home, as it is in this unfolding, is a place where something is discovered, founded, created, and/or developed. It is the beginning, center, and destination of poetic re-emergence, return, and resting. This poetic home allows the space for nesting and rebuilding. Bachelard (1994) connects the idea of nests to a hole or envelopment that can be used as armor or allow for many corners or "hiding places" (p. 91). It is a way of multiplying images or identities within a nesting refuge.

While poets may seek the collective comfort of a nesting refuge, Rilke (1962) reminds us in *Letters to a Young Poet* that "Nobody can counsel and help you… there is only one single way. Go into yourself" (p. 16). Rilke further directs a young poet to seek to express her everyday life; speak of her sorrows as well as her desires; hold a belief in (some sort of) beauty; write and speak with love and sincerity; express her feelings, dreams, and her memories.

The adolescent poets in the Poetic Eight, like all poets, are called to bear both the burden and the greatness of the expression of their feelings. As the poet's inner feelings and life grow, they lead to new insights, clarity, and truths. The lived experience cannot be forced or hurried but must unfold naturally like the phenomenological research process itself. The lived experiences and phenomenological research process charge us all to walk through sorrow, joy, and remembrances to come home to ourselves and venture into our homesteading. The members of the Poetic Eight have, individually and collectively, walked through their remembrances and homecoming. As they arrive at their homesteading, they re-enter the space of the living and are charged by life as well as their memories.

As I reflect on the pedagogical insight of this work, I seek to illustrate the "showing" of what it means to teach in a culturally responsive manner. So rather than identify technical instructional strategies to help others teach in this way, I am offering significant examples through pedagogical statements for possible practice. As a culturally responsive educator and poet/writer, I envisioned a poetry program that would create the space for all of the voices of the African American adolescent girl participants to be uncovered and heard. Some of the poetic unfolding that occurred throughout the creation and facilitation of this poetry program required an intense level of engagement from me as an educator, writer, researcher, designer, facilitator, and co-participant.

Writing and reading poetry and literature during or through the process of grief and loss can require an especially intense level of support and presence as a poetry facilitator (Hynes & Hynes-Berry, 1994). Therefore, at various times, I touched base with or informally consulted other professionals or mentors (academic/educational, spiritual, artistic, and counseling professionals). I also consulted a variety of texts, poetry books, readings, journals, formal classes, trainings, and workshops I have taken or taught, along with my own writings (poetry and journal entries), inner guide, and lived experiences.

Poetic Ethics

I caution educators against creating a culturally responsive poetry group without first exploring and examining their own professional and personal backgrounds, lived experiences, and comfort with writing, reading, and actively listening to culturally responsive poetry. educators bring their own pedological strengths, academic backgrounds, narratives, lived experiences, and beliefs to the forefront in creating a culturally responsive poetry group. I utilize my lived experience, Bachelor of Arts in human development, training in therapeutic poetry, Master of Education in Special Education, PhD in Curriculum and Instruction, experience as a poet, writer, and teacher, as well as a mother.

In my study and work, I made a very important distinction between creating a poetry therapy group and creating a culturally responsive poetry group. My study is *not* designed to provide a model for a therapy group. My study is designed solely to provide an educational model for a culturally responsive poetry group. In creating such a group, it is critical to make the distinction between a poetry therapy group and a poetry writing group. While poetry can be experienced as cathartic, healing, or even "therapeutic," the purpose of this study was to provide African American adolescent girls with the opportunity to explore their naming through writing poetry.

Participants in my study wrote from their imaginations, sense of activism and social justice, past personal experiences, and vicarious experiences of family members, friends, and society. None of my participants unfolded their writings from either personal or present circumstances of violence, self-injurious behavior, or violent or injurious behavior from or toward others. It is absolutely critical to note that if students/participants report/disclose being abused, the abuse must be reported as mandated by law. For example, when Keisha disclosed that she was raped by a classmate, school personnel immediately reported the incident to the authorities.

In my poetry groups over the years, students who displayed behavior that I believed to be inappropriate, inconsistent, unmanageable, escalating, or unsafe for themselves, poetry group members, or me were either not selected to participate in an educational poetry group or were not allowed to continue to participate in the poetry group.

As a special education teacher and case manager, the school environments that were most conducive to a culturally responsive poetry group were the ones in which I was able to work with a team of professionals. Team members in these settings consisted of an administrator, general education teacher, school psychologist or social worker, pupil personnel worker, school counselor, and parent/guardian. However, in order to maintain trust within the poetry group, it is critical that the student/participant be consulted or provide her consent if the teacher/facilitator intends to share her writing with others unless the student is in danger or is a danger to others. I not only highly recommend collaborating with other professionals, I deem it essential (particularly when working with students who are struggling, have experienced trauma, or have special needs; Bacon, 2009, 2022).

Creating Clearings in the Wilderness

I actively pursued, carved out, and created the support and connections that in a holistic educational system should be in place and readily available to educators but often are not. Generally, in the field of education, we are called upon to wear numerous hats. Yet in many schools, the ability and support to collaborate with other professionals and experts in the field (especially creatively), even before a student goes into crisis, are not available or considered valuable (Dance, 2002; Kauffmann, 1999; Bacon, 2009). Educators who enter into this space of human connection and poetic engagement risk criticism from some administrators, testing stakeholders, and colleagues, as well as risk fatigue, burnout, or eventual numbness from the demands that this practice of engagement requires (particularly if unsupported and working in isolation; Dean, Salend & Taylor, 1993). Therefore, having a support system is critical as isolation easily seeps into work that should generate connection.

As teachers, we often lament about the fact that while we seek to educate and connect with our students holistically, the current system inhibits such opportunities. We are programmed to teach to the test, teach without feeling, and to work without genuine support and in isolation. Human connections do not translate, for schools, into making adequate yearly progress (AYP) or passing the HSA (high school state assessments), or other standardized assessments.

In my experience, poetry programs or student-generated learning often do not fit into the curriculum or even a ninety-minute block class schedule. Some programs are run by outside organizations or community poets for a limited amount of time because teachers are unable to allot additional time, have limited resources, or are already overstretched. The workday is long, the paperwork often all consuming, and the tasks, expectations and obligations of teachers seem never-ending (Bacon, 2009; Dance, 2002; Dean, Salend & Taylor, 1993).

My poetry programs have occurred either at lunch or after school because that was the only time when we were able to meet regularly without "interrupting instruction." Students who experience grief have diverse needs or want to address issues of empowerment rarely have creative outlets built into the fabric of traditional schools (Bacon, 2009, 2016; Dance, 2002; Kauffmann, 1999). I have spoken with other devoted teachers and educators who have shared, practically with tears in their eyes, that they wish they could run this type of program. It is not their lack of compassion, concern, or devotion that keeps them from doing so but rather the lack of support, demands from the county, administration, and high-stakes assessments.

Safekeeping: Protecting the Heart

"Much of the pedagogical and political work of forming self and communities, by youth, takes place well outside the borders of schooling" (Weis & Fine, 2000, p. xi). The "interest meeting" for my study serves as such a confirmation of youth attempting to connect outside of classroom borders. During the interest meeting for my poetry group, students arrived after school individually. in twos and threes, in clusters, and in droves. They arrived after the door was closed to the warmly insulated, brightly lit English classroom until the room contained twenty-three interested, self-identified African American adolescent girl poets. And once the interest meeting was over, a few more girls arrived the following day, when I was not present, to drop off poetry samples and inquire if they could still join.

While I was overjoyed at the response to my poetry group and the powerful ways in which the invitation spoke to the need for African American adolescent girls to express themselves through poetic voice, I recognized the responsibility for us as educators, community members, curriculum designers, stakeholders, administrators, and the like to create a system that supports and staffs such programs regularly. How can we create space where all of our students who want and need an outlet are able to find one safely within the school setting? The task feels somewhat daunting, but we must undergo it (Lynn et al., 2010).

I am reminded of the writings of culturally responsive scholars, such as Lisa Delpit and Joanne Kilgour Dowdy's *The Skin That We Speak: Thoughts on Language and Culture in the Classroom* (2002). The authors unfold the development of self-esteem by African American students who have their linguistic expression and culture honored in the classroom. Delpit further offers the lived experience of her daughter, Maya, who felt like an outcast in her predominantly White school. However, when Maya transferred to a predominantly African American school, which supported her culture and voice, her self-esteem soared along with her verbal expression. Delpit and Kilgour Dowdy's work surrounding linguistic expression and cultural vernacular connects to the lived experiences of the Poetic Eight uncovering and maintaining their power to name who they are. The Poetic Eight uncovers and maintains their sense of empowerment through their unadulterated poetic writings and creative expression.

As a society, when we silence students' authentic selves and cultures, we lose their truths, their stories, their power, their voices— we lose them. What we also lose when we silence students' authentic selves is us. We are linked to our students, our community, and our society by our humanness; we cannot realize our visions and voices without a collective consciousness (Bacon, 2009, 2017; Dean, et al., 1993; Freire, 1994, 2000; Irvine, 2003; O'Donohue, 1997).

Eighth grade poetry participants in Wiseman's (2004) study shared that in traditional classrooms they did not have the same (positive) relationship with their teachers once they entered high school. Participants in my study expressed a similar feeling of disconnection from their high school teachers. Therefore, it was imperative for me during my study to establish a relationship with each group member to offset their negative high school experiences and build trust and a sense of community. Positive relationships were paramount to the success of my poetry program.

Culturally Responsive Pedagogy: Pathway to the Poet's Heart

In creating a culturally responsive poetry group, three crucial topics are brought forth through the unfolding of my study: culturally responsive pedagogy, literacy, and phenomenology grounded in Black feminism.

In maintaining the tradition of culturally responsive pedagogy, Black feminism, and phenomenology, I invite teachers to allow room and space for students' self-generated works and topics in poetry. What calls to your students? What do they seek to read, discuss, and experience? What stories would be unwritten if they did not write them?

I modeled my expectation of positive and supportive interactions between group members through my interactions with my participants. I actively listened to participants and included "check-ins" and discussions during every meeting. I displayed respect for participants' ideas, feelings, and thoughts through verbal affirmation and validation. I also encouraged each student to have a voice in my poetry group. During each poetry group session, I provided time for participants to read several poems. If a participant did not have an opportunity to read her work, I frequently remained for an additional half hour (as allowed by the after school program) to hear her readings and engage in discussions.

Like many culturally responsive educators, I often viewed myself and was viewed by the girls as an "other mother" (Bacon, 2022; Irvine, 2003). My role as an "other mother" helped to solidify my accountability to group members and to encourage each of them to establish a certain level of accountability to their "poetry sisters." In addition to creating and facilitating poetry sessions, I checked on the girls' grades, listened to their stories, provided feedback, touched base with their families as needed, celebrated birthdays and graduations, contacted them between meetings via email or phone, and provided them with my contact information to call or email me. I also encouraged the girls to check in with one another between meetings.

In my study, relationships and communication were the foundation for creating and maintaining trust. Prior to the first day, I began to establish trust through modeling personal engagement and self-disclosure. I also provided a brief biography for my participants and shared some of my own poetry writing such as "Strong and Sassy." I began on the first day with an introduction of the program. I reviewed student letters, guidelines, and expectations. Following my guidelines and expectations for the group, I inquired about their expectations. I encouraged communication and openly inquired about their definitions of trust. I asked the girls what trust meant to them. I asked for their ideas about the ways in which trust could be established in the group and conflicts could be resolved.

The Poetic Eight and I came to a consensus that trust would be evaluated in terms of open and honest communication, the showing of kindness, and respecting privacy. We also agreed that trust could not flourish with teasing or "putting down" the ideas, writing, or feelings of group members or the facilitator. We also agreed that talking about one another in a negative way to other members of the group or outside of the group would constitute a violation of trust. Because communication and trust are essential, I created a lesson plan for the first day with the goal of building these components.

Since positive relationships were deemed to be imperative, during the second meeting I created a lesson plan to begin cultivating relationships within the group. I began by continuing the discussion on trust and followed up with a candid conversation about friendship and sisterhood. I asked, "What makes a good friend?" I also asked, "What does friendship look like?" and "What is sisterhood?" In addition to working as a group, students worked in pairs to establish more individual communication. Relationships, communication, and trust created a clearing to "Emergence of the I Ams" (Bacon, 2009, Chapter Four).

Teaching Applications for the Poetic Heart

I firmly believe that even teachers who are "non-poets" are capable of successfully creating and facilitating a culturally responsive poetry group. However, teachers must be willing to take the risks that they ask of their students. Teachers/facilitators must lead from the heart, engage, and participate in poetry writing, readings, and discussions with openness. Although teachers might need to adjust my study design and format to accommodate their work environments, schedules, or comfort level, the elements of positive communication, trust, and accountability must remain consistent for success. In adapting my design for a poetry group during class time, it is important to recognize that some secondary schools operate on a ninety-minute "block" schedule (where classes meet less frequently for longer periods of time), while others might operate daily on a fifty- or sixty-minute schedule. Therefore, teachers might need to shorten or expand a lesson.

In my poetry study, I included ice breakers, writing activities, and discussions that built upon and fostered exploration and imagination. Into the fabric of this study, I built time during each meeting for students to share topics they wanted to discuss, bringing forth what was on their minds and in their hearts (Gorman, 1999; Rothstein, 1993). I also had them lead and facilitate poetry segments, activities, and discussions.

In order for students to uncover their power to name who they really are through writing, they must be allowed to write what is of interest or relevant to them. Furthermore, in my study the empowerment process unfolded in four stages: writing, reading/speaking (their poems, stories, and truths), being heard (having their voices received by listening ears), and hearing others (creating the collective and reciprocal experience through active listening; Levin, 1989). In this process, even if the lived experiences are not one's own, there is an element of recognition. Recognition offers engagement for the listener as she connects with her own experiences, observations, reflections, desires or concerns (such as activism or social justice), or sense of what is felt or known "in their bodies" (Levin, 1989, p. 102). Recognition provides the space to develop or reflect on emerging themes within the group, individual experience, or writing patterns (Hynes & Hynes-Berry, 1994).

Following recognition, exploration of the meaning and feelings of the writer and listeners is critical. This process is supported and nurtured by the facilitator and upheld by the group (Hynes & Hynes-

Berry, 1994). In my group, the adolescent girls offered tremendous insight, guidance, and encouragement to members as peers, co-facilitators, and anam caras. My unfolding process and program design was brought forth and provided mainly by the lived experiences of my participants. Although their experiences are unique, they represent the collective and universal voices of African American adolescent girl poets. Therefore, as an educator, I seek to provide other educators and researchers with the tools and insight for creating their own poetry groups with the recognition that the groups will be as varied and distinctive as the participants themselves. I also provide a facilitation model and lesson plans to assist in the formation of a culturally responsive poetry group.

Ideally poetry groups should remain small. I suggest 8–12 participants. My first poetry group (discussed in Section Two) and my recent poetry group consisted of eight members. Small groups allow participants more time to write, read, and discuss their poetry. Smaller groups also seem to provide the space for students to become better acquainted with one another and the facilitator. However, poetry groups can be constructed for large classes. Even in a class of thirty, students can assume leadership roles. Large groups can also be divided into groups of 3 4 four (allowing the participant number of 8–12 to be maintained). Students are also able to serve as facilitators. Facilitators and participants may be rotated to allow students to build relationships.

As a special education teacher, I often used the co-teaching model for my poetry groups during class. In my inclusion classes (consisting of special education and general education students), the general education teacher and I facilitated groups simultaneously. In my self-contained classes (consisting of all special education students), I facilitated poetry groups with the para-educator (teacher's assistant).

My poetry groups are designed to uncover and maintain participants' power. Students are also empowered by being supported in creating their own poetry groups. Teachers may remain connected with students by serving as sponsors or consultants for student-facilitated poetry groups and programs instead of assuming the role of facilitator. During my last meeting with the Poetic Eight, we divided up tasks, and each participant selected a role such as facilitating, sending out meeting notices, or bringing snacks. Student leadership roles in poetry groups provide additional opportunities for students to uncover and maintain their voices. Participants' power to name in my study allowed them to explore and use their voices of resistance for the purpose of emancipation.

Freire (1994, 2000) charges society to develop literacy practices as a means of creating resistance and empowerment. Resistance and empowerment through literacy are especially important to African American adolescent girls as members of underrepresented groups (African Americans, girls and young women, individuals with special needs, or urban students). My study provided a deep poetic rendering of the experiences of my participants. My poetry program was student centered and offered high-interest material that allowed students to make connections to literacy and their lived experiences while constructing meaning.

The Poetic Art of Fusion: Phenomenology and Black Feminism

My study brings the voices, presence, and lived experiences of African American adolescent girls and women into visibility. My study, Culturally Responsive Poetry: The Lived Experience of African American Adolescent Girl Poets, increases the diversity of materials researched and written about and by African American adolescent girls and women. This study is designed to provide diversity and multiculturalism within the practice of phenomenology by fusing a Black feminist perspective with phenomenology.

The Poetic Eight has repeated Audre Lorde's (2007) call that for Black women and adolescent girls writing is a necessity and not a luxury. Writing based on urgency and necessity is created whether it is invited or requested because it is the path that leads from suffering to wholeness. It is also the path that opens up the poet's heart and allows her to exist fully from behind the mask to beyond it.

I discovered that for some members of the Poetic Eight writing, is literally the substitute for bleeding out tears. These are the tears that did not run from their tear ducts but rather ran from their veins. Writing thaws the numbness to bring feeling back to the damaged hands that clasped the pen when they could grasp nothing else (Bacon, 2009; Hurston, 1942; Walker, 1997).

My research has revealed the urgent need for a holistic design in education that includes the lived experiences, writings, and voices of African American girls and women in the curriculum rather than exclusively in afterschool programs. It is a place where these experiences are not merely provided a quick glance during Black History Month or Women's History Month. The curriculum design is fused with culturally responsive pedagogy that does not further marginalize the lives of African American girls and women as a footnote (Hull, Scott & Smith, 1982; Sheftall, 1995). It is necessary to have a curriculum design that is centered upon lived experiences, co-authorship and humanity. In order to resurrect change and make audible the voices of silenced African American girls and Black women, writing poetry must be viewed as a necessity rather than a luxury.

These urgent voices still call to me. They prompt me to stay in the in-between spaces to revisit homecoming and voicelessness and homesteading in joy once more. I seek to stay in this space to allow questions to surface as a researcher and as an educator. How will my future research allow me to bring the voices of my participants into the space of the curriculum? How can the educational curriculum be "broken" to be rebuilt? My research calls me to continue to uncover more voices of once invisible and silenced African American adolescent girls and Black women to be led to a resting place in homesteading that resides within and without the borders of schools and education.

I spent several years in the classroom as a special education teacher and case manager. I spent an additional year outside of the classroom as a special education department chairperson. I worked very closely with students in crisis who did not have outlets in the traditional school setting. However, this poetry program took place after school once I was no longer an employee of the public school system. Rather, I was a full-time doctoral candidate and a university supervisor. Working with high school students after school and working with student-teachers during the day helped me to remain connected to the pulse of the school system.

Having one foot in both worlds reminded me of the necessity to ensure that student-teachers had the awareness, knowledge, and skills to become culturally responsive educators. I reminded my student-teachers to hear the voices of their students. I sought to make them aware of the invisibility and silences created by marginalization. I also encouraged my student-teachers to know their students well enough to hear what their students did not say. I echo the voices of Black feminists' scholars and writers Gloria T. Hull, Patricia Bell Scott, and Barbara Smith (1982) and seek to be guided by my research in creating a curriculum design, teacher preparation class, writing project and publication that represent the voices of African American adolescent girl poets.

Engaging in my poetry study with high school students allowed me to remain connected to the process. I was reminded of the needs, thoughts, and challenges of young people. I was also reminded of the demands of teaching. Yet, no longer being employed by the public school system provided me with the freedom and autonomy I did not have as a classroom teacher. Not being employed by the county, I was liberated from bureaucracy, mandated state assessments, policymakers and the central office. I was free to do what I loved the most and found to be the most beneficial—work with the children.

However, I was not freed from financial responsibility. I was required to fund the program and provide resources, and to do so as a volunteer. Many poetry and art programs, as my program, are not funded at all by the school system or given limited funding or phased out (Wiseman, 2004, Garran, 2004). Editors Gloria T. Hull, Patricia Bell Scott, and Barbara Smith (in *All the Women are White, All the Blacks are Men, But Some of Us Are Brave*, 1982) offer that visions of Black feminists writers, researchers, and culturally responsive educators must be funded and supported. The editors emphasize providing funds for individual research projects of Black women scholars, as well as funding teacher preparation programs and curricular materials. They also reveal the need for funding Black women's studies courses, which I suggest would be enhanced by the inclusion of writings by student participants.

As I rest in the imagination of homesteading within the borders of schools and education, I see a flicker of light for future researchers. In creating a culturally responsive poetry model, culturally responsive pedagogy and literacy must be intertwined. Culturally responsive literacy practices may increase students' voices and sense of empowerment while enhancing their oral communication skills, written expression, and reading fluency (accuracy and speed) (Algozzine, O'Shea, & Obiakor, 2009). My study, however, is a phenomenological study guided by the lived experiences of writing poetry for African American adolescent girls to uncover the power to name who they really are. Therefore, my research was not designed to increase such literacy practices as reading fluency or writing mechanics. However, my study opens a space for future researchers in the area of culturally responsive poetry for the purpose of enhancing literacy skills. As I return to phenomenology, I move to a place of homesteading.

Poetic Homesteading

Homesteading provides a future home-place as well as an ending place (Casey, 1993). Homesteading brings some members of Poetic Eight from the confusion, despair and grief over death and abandonment to the remembrance of love. Love rests in the heart of the divine, themselves, each other, memories of their mothers and mother figures. Poetic Eight's stories are intertwined with the branches of philosophers, Black feminist writers, poets, story tellers, and educators. As writers, they overlap and move between one another's poetic consciousness and voices as they uncover themselves, carve out new identities and names, and shed old ones that no longer serve them. False identities are shed that keep them grief stricken or keep them from being strong Black women who cry, feel, and speak their truths.

The poetry group offers a space for writing in community and connection rather than in isolation. It is a place to be heard and understood. This poetic space serves not only as a means to express the necessity of writing for African American adolescent girls but a place to write stories that may not have otherwise existed. Stories and experiences, once written, are powerful enough to leap from the pages as "living words" that breathe life back into the body and heart of the writer. Living words allow the listener also to experience this journey as rhapsode and griotte but, more important, as a part of a culture of humanity.

Uncovering the power to name who you really are is as much about what the young women and adolescent girls name themselves through their pen names as it is about stepping into those names as poets. By stepping into themselves and their many names, they also embody their power with wit and wisdom. Each member of the Poetic Eight, in her own unique way, creates her own voice and power. Sometimes, that voice is heard primarily through her silence.

Emerging Responsibility of the Poets to One Another

> It is interesting to cut yourself into pieces once in a while, and wait to see if the fragments will sprout.
> (Eliot, in Vendler, 1998, p. viii)

T.S. Eliot was a Harvard graduate finishing his PhD in philosophy when he left Harvard to spend a year at Oxford University in England, never to return. While he finished his dissertation, he turned more seriously to poetry, which he had written since his senior year in college, and eventually won the Nobel Prize for literature. As Heidegger is credited for transforming phenomenology, Eliot is credited for transforming modern literature (Vendler, 1998).

Eliot wrote, as many writers do, to impart his imagination and interpretation of the world. This interpretation and imagination have also been said to be a mark of the greatest writers who "impose" their imagination on others (Vendler, 1998, p. ix). However, there is often a fine line between writers offering, inviting, imagining, inventing, interpreting, and imposings, which in my study, I seek to distinguish. There are times when my role and the roles of my co-participants as interpreters, truth sayers, and writers blend or become blurred. These are the spaces that also open up to the possibilities of many truths, meanings, and names that are fluid and transformative for the writer and the listener.

Interpretation is another profound power uncovered in poetry in which we as writers and listeners connect the poems to our lived experiences or the stories of those we are familiar with and have yet to be told. As we are called upon to fulfill our responsibilities as poets and writers to speak for ourselves, as well as for others who cannot speak, it is with recognition that such speaking may also be an imposition by the writer on those we have written about or on their behalf. However, to shrink from this challenge is not an option; nor is silence or timidity in this space of poetic expression and interpretation. So, it is with conviction and fire that the Poetic Eight and I offer our voices and our truths.

The story of Eliot reveals the path of a writer who in public concealed his inner sorrow from the world, but through his poetry, concealed nothing. This is the path of writers shown from Keisha's declaration of "You Don't Know Me" in Section One to Mishaps' "Suffocation" in Section Four. I acknowledge the places in which Mishaps, Blue, Divine Diva, KiRe, Queen of Hearts, and Lenash "concealed nothing" in their poetry. I also acknowledge the places where Family and Camille maintained a public concealing of their feelings.

In my own pedagogical homesteading, I seek to balance remembrances with repeating the process and practice unfolded throughout this study. However, I do not seek to be redundant to the reader. Instead, as I look toward voice, silence, and future clearings, I make space for the voices and feelings that remained muted or inaudible in my participants' stories and writings. I listen for the silences. I seek to hear the spaces where ontological (fulfilling) silences and epistemological (knowing) silences become voiceless silences.

Voice through Silence

While this study is guided by uncovering and maintaining the power for adolescent girls to name who they really are and find their way home to themselves and their voices, one of the most powerful tools for voice is silence. The silences of Family and Camille, who have the courage to reveal their shyness to the group, continue to prompt them, in their own way, to remain engaged and present. Their stories are often told beneath, "There's nothing new" or "I have nothing interesting to say." O'Donohue (1997) reminds us that it is beneath a smile that the hidden world of experiences is brought forth. Moreover, in our facial expressions, maybe sometimes more than in our words, possibilities and pathways to our hearts are created and illuminated. As with the listening ear, "If we knew how to read the faces of others, we would be able to decipher the mysteries of their life stories" (O' Donohue, p. 39).

Phenomenology allows us to illuminate the mysteries and intricacies of the human condition. Silence is often more active and responsive than voice. Active silence calls for the ability to be present, offers reverence in a sacred poetic space, and ignites imagination (Steiner, 1989). As an interpreter or rhapsode in this study, I have been called to decipher and communicate meaning for many of the poems of my co-participants. Gadamer (2004) reminds us that interpretation, in a certain sense, is re-creation. Re-creation is not an interpretation of the "creative act but of the created work" (p. 119). Moreover, re-creation allows the interpreter to find meaning in the creative work.

According to Steiner (1989), an interpreter acts as a translator not only between languages but between cultures. Through this study, I seek to interpret, when necessary, the voices and poetic culture of African American adolescent girls with authenticity and integrity. Through these experiences, it is not only the work of the girls that is felt and encountered but the human voice of another. Steiner (1989) uses the term "answerability" to mean the following: "The authentic experience of understanding, when we are spoken to by another human being or by a poem, is one of responding responsibility" (p. 8). He writes about the creation of the ideal society as one in which there are imagination and meaningful exchanges. In this utopian society, deep creative intellect is valued. Discourse and interpretation are not valued and offered by outsiders who seek to merely criticize poetry, art, and music without being producers of such creative expression. Rather, interpretation, discussion, and even critique are offered through the insight of a fellow creator as an insider. This creation and exchange occur only when critics, judges, and reviewers are not the impositional voice in this space.

Gadamer (2004) reminds us that achievements in the human sciences are never outdated. Rather, the subject matter remains significant when it is properly portrayed by the researcher. Thus, studies acquire life from the way they are presented and experienced. As an insider in this study and sacred poetic space, I embrace this phenomenological ideal and hermeneutic exploration as a Black woman writer. I have many shared lived experiences and stories with my co-participants, as well as many unique ones. As a writer, my ability to ignite their poetic voices occurred by creating a safe space for poets to speak and write their feelings and experiences with truth(s). As an interpreter, my "responding responsibility" is unraveling and writing renderings with the intention of embodying the hope, joy, rage, and love that the poets have spilled onto the pages and read in the group in earnestness and conviction.

Future Clearings to Silences Still Muted

At this point in the journey, we see that while we carry the voices, legacies, and stories of our mothers, mother figures, and ancestors, we also acknowledge that some of their unfinished business or untold stories will not be ours to complete. For each member of the Poetic Eight to find her own voice, fulfill her own dreams, and reveal her own truths, she must also step from behind the shadows. Following the path of others has covered and enveloped these young African American poets and, at times, even stifled or suffocated them. Yet, they have grown into themselves and embarked on a journey of living and writing their own stories.

As I reflect on the growth of members of the Poetic Eight and their transition into womanhood, I am reminded of Alice Walker's (1983) naming of Black feminists as "womanists." She offers the name from the "black folk expression" of mothers to girls whose behaviors are deemed to be "womanish" or beyond their years, behavior often seen as outrageous, willful, or courageous (p. xi).

The members of Poetic Eight, throughout my study, offer their voices and naming(s) as adolescent girls who acknowledge the struggles of transitioning from girlhood to womanhood. Moreover, they offer their poetry, lived experiences, stories, imagination, and voices of resistance with "womanish" willfulness and courage beyond their years. And as Poetic Eight embraces their homesteading and growing voices, they move into Walker's further naming of a "womanist." Walker (2003) offers the next naming of a "womanist" as a woman who either appreciates or prefers women's culture, emotional flexibility (from tears to laughter), and strength. A "womanist" is committed to wholeness (in women and men) and humanity. Moreover, a "womanist" loves "the Spirit," struggle, life, and, most of all, her full self (p. xi).

As the members of the Poetic Eight acknowledge their spirit, struggle, lives, and full selves, I acknowledge the group closure process in this transition. I invite discussions around the group concluding and ask each member to make a list of resources, adults, or peers whom she could talk with, confide in, or share her writing. Group closure also consists of celebrating and affirming the young women's transition into adulthood and/or college.

During our final meeting, I organized a graduation party for Mishaps, KiRe, and Queen of Hearts. This acknowledgement of closure and transition was expanded to include all of the young women by going around the room and sharing positive and distinctive qualities about each member. Closure was also extended to family members of the Poetic Eight, who provided food for the graduation party in honor of the senior women's accomplishments. After the celebration, I met with the remaining members of the Poetic Eight. I invited them to continue their writing and work with one another by supporting the establishment of a student-run poetry group. I also offered to continue to serve as a consultant.

The process of group closure is further illuminated by the Poetic Eight's growing voices. I conclude my study with the acknowledgment of my participants' transition from girlhood to womanhood through their final reflections and poetry writing. Through their reflections, they continue to reveal their transformation from African American adolescent girl poets to Black women writers.

Growing Voices

> I'm doing this stuff for me. I got to the point where I realized that I got to this stuff because I was putting my effort into it. (Blue, in Bacon, 2009, p. 297)

> Sometimes you have to satisfy yourself. First quarter I had a 3.6 next quarter I had a 3.2 But I was satisfied. I still made the honor roll and that satisfies.
> (Queen of Hearts, in Bacon, 2009, p. 297)

This study is a story of being fully alive. The poetic expressions on these pages have been about revealing sorrow and grief, bringing forth joy, truth, and ridiculous shrieking ("why are they laughing so loud in public??!" kind of heartfelt laughter). Truth is revealed in the belief that there is a dawn after the despair. And the light of dawn is so beautiful and clear that you can look directly into it. Looking into the light of dawn did not take our sight, as I unfolded in Section Two, but provided us with it.

As I stated in the preface of my study, culturally responsive poetry is the unearthing of African American adolescents' self-definition through a process of naming (to call forth their own names and multiple identities). It involves poetry writing as both individual and collective efforts by and for African American adolescent girls, a bold and passionate declaration of self-identity.

Individually Camille has unearthed many names throughout my study. Through her writings and discussions, she has called forth her names and identity(ies) as: Camille, Preacher's Daughter, Queen of the Nile, My Brother's Keeper, Secrecy, and A Person with Very Little to Say. Mishaps has uncovered her power beginning with her suffocation and closing with her emerging happiness. She has unearthed such names throughout these chapters as: Mishaps, A Bitter Person ("but not as much"), Bold, Whole, New, God's Gift, Known, Dead Souls, and Happy.

Divine Diva has uncovered her power to name herself beginning with her declaration as a Divine Diva. She further defines herself as A Child of God, Always the Good Girl, Someone Who Can Do Anything She Sets Her Mind To, and a Burden. Queen of Hearts begins her naming journey with writing as a Queen of Hearts and Mender of Other People's Problems and Hearts. As she continues along her journey, her voice of resistance also emerges through her declaration as: True, Next Freedom Writer, and Black Panther.

Blue's naming began with her delving into her emotions. Uncovering her power to name led her to defining Blue as a Normal Color. Blue also offered her internally defined names as Blue Jay, Fire, and Black Power. Lenash's naming called out with the power to claim herself as A Nigerian Woman, Symphony, and Lenash. KiRe asserted her naming as I Know Who I Am, KiRe, Lively Spirits, Everything, and

Sometimes Unsure. Family recognizes her naming in this poetic unfolding as Me. While she has not claimed her names as Hope and Honesty, she writes that she has them within her. My participants name themselves the Poetic Eight. In their collective naming, the girls recognize their identities as poets and as members of a united group.

The journey of the African American adolescent girl poets of my study reflects the beauty and angst of self-discovery, identity, and self-definition. Phenomenology unfolds the poets' lived experiences, deepening the meaning of each writing experience as the process reflects not only the essence and meaning of the poems but the essence of the poet.

This work in phenomenology allows us, as participants and as researchers, to explore and uncover. In phenomenology, we often ask more questions than assert answers; we change and constantly evolve. The process of inquiry, change, and poetic revelation is often where joy enters—not only in this methodology but in our individual and collective hearts. Walker, Lorde, Freire, and Steiner write of literacy, language, and voice as tools for change, resistance, power, freedom, and wholeness. Consciousness and empowerment are not measured in high-stake assessments or revealed through rote memorization. Rather, they are unfolded in my phenomenological study through the writing, listening, and truth saying that are connected to our lives. The final reflections of the Poetic Eight provide such insight as they declare, "All of us have grown whether the outside sees it or not."

> I've enjoyed having people understand me. Even though I'm still working on my life, I've had so much fun getting to know new people. I learned you can write what you feel it doesn't have to be about the topic. You can write what your heart tells you to write. I love being in the poetry club because I can let out all my emotions and not worry about people judging me. (Divine Diva, in Bacon, 2009, p. 299)

> It was fun and a good experience... overwhelmed with good. The experience made me realize the [potential] everyone has in new things. (Blue, in Bacon, 2009, p.300)

> [I'm] not trying to slice you but seeing someone like you, [a] successful Black woman professional, talented, with her head on straight, etc who can deal with estrogen means it's possible. I know there were some days in the beginning that we came in

here there were attitudes. But you dealt with it. And still came into our school twice a week not just emails and you talked, and you actually asked, and cared. I think everybody should do this...

We accomplished a lot. Everybody, all of us have grown whether the outside sees it or not. Wow, I have friends (now) that are girls and are cool. That are actually decent people. I wish I could have gotten to something like this earlier (this was her last year in high school)

How I feel about leaving:
Waaaaaah... Exhale
Waaaahhhhh...Inhale
Wahhhhhhh..Inhale
Waahhh... inhale...Exhale
Waaaahhhhhh!!!
Okay, I'm finished 09!
(KiRe, in Bacon, 2009, p. 300)

I'm speechless I completely don't know what to say. I wish It could be a little longer... Naw maybe, it was one of the best experiences I've ever had and it helped me to grow. It took out hate and put in happiness it took away [doubt] and replaced it with hope. "I will miss everyone I love poetry...
I am every page in every word. I am every tear in every joy...
(Mishaps, in Bacon, 2009, p. 300)

Final Poetic Reflections

During this process, there were times when traveling this road as a researcher that I could not escape the occasional glimpse of a bumper sticker reminding me that, "All who wander are not lost." And it is with this recognition that I acknowledge that it is the path of wandering and wondering with a purpose that allowed me to reach out to others and to also bring myself home. This dissertation came through me like a birth. It initially caused suffering and great anguish before the catharsis (cleansing) and process of letting go. It has been a dream fulfilled, a divine thought, an inspiration answered, a questioning, a path of many blended into one, a truth, a searching, and a finding.

I began by looking outwardly, starting with the experiences of others from the nursing home to "These Black Kids" to Keisha to Blue,

Mishaps, and the Poetic Eight, only to find that at the end of the journey I had uncovered my own power through writing. This project ranged through places of my being an activities coordinator, a poetry therapy student, a special educator, a survivor, an African American woman, a mentor, a writer, and in more recent years, a professor and administrator, and now a mother, to be uncovered. I wanted from time to time to stop writing. But when the labor pains of creation hit, I came to understand that it must be born. And when it was ready, there was nothing that I could or would do to halt its entry into the world.

In the writings of each participant, I have supported getting this work "done" in ways that empowered the adolescent girls and provided the space for them to tell their stories or re-create them (and themselves) if they so chose/choose. In some ways, this study and research process has been a partial death for me in order to be reborn. I, too, have uncovered the power to name myself as a Black woman writer.

As I reflect on this journey, I acknowledge the fact that education and writing are among my greatest joys. Education and writing have also been my outlet for my highest truth and an expression of purest love. As this study comes to an end, I recognize that this experience has encompassed my greatest truth, joy, and love.

Speaking to My Heart

As I sit in this space I hear the echoes of my heart. There are whispers all around from the voices of the girl I once was, the adolescent I was becoming, and the woman I am now. I look out into the faces of these young women coming behind me and I wonder how it is possible that students, I only met a short time ago, can speak the echoes of my heart?

How is it that they have bonded as they have and at such an early age speak the truths that even as adults, we often do not have the courage to utter? Why is it that their voices mirror so many dimensions of my life as their present and my past memories? They speak and answer questions that are not only of their experiences but of the women who wrote before them and the girls who will write after them.

I imagine, on some level, this must be the face of motherhood. To look into your past and to hope for all that is good for your daughters'/children's futures. And while they speak my heart there is a comfort in knowing that they speak the echoes of their own hearts with their own voices. And they will now carry with them the memories of each other and visions of their tomorrows.

(Bacon, reflection, 2009, pp. 302–303)

No Longer Blue

Now 31, Blue returns to this space to take her place as a Black woman and holder of knowledge and stories. Rather than interpret the stories and poems of others, she offers her own adult voice to her adolescent poetry.

I open this final section and conversation with Blue by reading her poem by her request.

> Look to the sky, and I still don't understand what's going on. Like a repeating song, singing, 'Mom, Mommy, come and find me' but I haven't found me dealing with insecurities. Pain gushes like blood from a wound, feeling like a balloon, thoughts and pain. I want to go insane, and still I look to the sky feeling high on this drug of pain and still don't understand what's going on in my veins. A blood boil from blood pressure. Not having my mother is why I wonder, 'Why am I here?' Hearing rolling thunder. Wonder. Wonder. But still don't understand what's going on?"

Blue: Well, where do I begin? It was just a fresh wound without a band aid I would say. So, it was me coming to realize that this person that I admired so much and loved so much was not there physically. It was hard for me to understand what exactly I was feeling and basically expressing how I felt with words of thunder and all the pain. It allowed me to really express how I felt at that time. I was convinced but these words made me understand how I felt if that makes sense.

Jennifer Bacon: Yeah, it absolutely does. Sometimes it's hard to say it, but sometimes in the process of writing it and then you even get to step back and look at it and be like, "Oh, this is what I was feeling. I can just put it out on the page." And that's one of the things about poetry specifically too because it's pretty concise. You're using these powerful words, but it's not super long. It just gets to the emotion pretty quickly.

Blue: Yes. It does.

Jennifer Bacon: If it's okay with you before we do any more of the reflection questions, I want to be sure to also bring in your second poem and this one you wrote in 2008. This is one of the poems that I really find most touching because we did a lot of writing back then around grief and loss. On some level, everybody in the group was going through, a sense of grief and loss And then you and one of the other participants in particular you both lost your moms in high school. So, that process of writing through it I think is something that really speaks to so many people who might not always be able to express that emotion of what it's like to lose your mother at such a young age. So, this one is, "I haven't cried like I needed to. I don't know what to cry about. I tend to get sad but nothing ever happens. Mainly people may have noticed that when I cry there's something really wrong with me. I never cry over little things or someone trying to hurt my feelings, but I know one day it will all come out. You will see what my life is really about."

Blue: I don't think I'm reading it correctly. I'm not getting the passion I used to.

Jennifer Bacon: Do you feel when you see this as passionately as you did before? How is this now? Because it's been, goodness, 14 years, right? Let me do that math real fast. How does it feel now when you look back and see your old work? Has everything come out? Because this, "But I know one day it will all come out." How does it feel for you?

Blue: Well, honestly, it makes me feel good because reading where I used to be and then where I am, it's been a tremendous transition. Because, like I said, you read this so much better than me but when I was actually reading my old poems, those two in particular, I didn't get the same feeling I did when I wrote it. And the reason why I feel like I did not is because I have grown. I have put together pieces of my life that I could not put together back then and I know so much now about grief. You know, what works for me may not work for everyone else, but how I cope and how I deal with it, and what things that I do to deal with it. I did continue to write, but I also did therapy. I also did counseling during college, because it became a thing where I felt like I was backpeddling in my emotions, because school can be very stressful. So, I feel so proud of myself.

Jennifer Bacon: Knowing all that you know now, and how hard you worked, and going to therapy and continuing with your writing and that you have made it passed so much of the grief and the sorrow. I think it can be a life process in some ways when we're looking at loss, especially something as significant as losing our moms. What would you say to yourself back then? What would you, 31-year-old Blue, say to junior and high school senior Blue?

Blue: Well, I would tell myself that expressing those feelings and never holding back inside and feeling those feelings is a part of dealing with grief in the healing process and it takes time. It does not come overnight. And to open your mind to doing things that will put you in a cheerful spirit when you're down like writing poetry, drawing, listening to music, anything that brings you pleasure.

Jennifer Bacon: Absolutely. Do you feel like, the part of the writing poetry and bringing joy, did it make a difference? Do you think that it was done with other girls, with other women in community? Do you think that helps at all with the grieving process or is it more of a one-on-one experience or a solo experience?

Blue: Oh, no. That helped tremendously because it made me feel like I'm not the only one going through this. How are other people dealing with it? How are other people coping? What are their ways to deal with this grief and this loss? It also opened my eyes to understanding that it was okay to be confused and not know what to do, because I wasn't the only one experiencing that. So, that felt so great. The group was… I still to this day talk about it with everyone I know. It was so awesome!

Jennifer Bacon: It was a pleasure to have such brilliant young minds all together and working on writing for the common good, too, because I remember you all wrote about grief and loss. You wrote about social justice issues. I think we had some poetry around domestic violence. That was back in the day when Chris Brown had beaten Rihanna, and so there were some poems around that. That consciousness was really uplifting and inspiring in so many ways.

Blue: Yes, very uplifting.

Jennifer Bacon: So, Blue, with that in mind, would you say in some ways this type of writing cycle is somewhat complete? Is there anything else with the writing that you would continue on the path of healing and loss?

Blue: Well, the whole interaction with other people I feel like is very important. For example, a lot of people that have struggled with drug abuse and alcohol abuse, they attend AA meetings for those situations. We don't really have a group just for grieving and healing besides going to a counselor. I feel like that was a part of my life. That became a part of me. That was my AA for me to express how I was feeling, how everyone felt the same, how they felt similar in their life.

Jennifer Bacon: I think that's such a wonderful way to describe it, beautiful. I have to ask you, what advice would you have for high school girls right now? They are contending with a lot, right? I mean, they've gone through a pandemic. We've seen the tragic loss of George Floyd in front of the whole world, the Black Lives Matter movement, #SayHerName. I mean, there's been so many important uprisings based on some of these tragedies and violence and isolation. So much going on in the world, so it's like negotiating a whole other space, isn't it?

Blue: Yes, my advice would be take your time with life. Never be in a rush. Follow your hopes and dreams. Never let anyone change who you are. Embrace your personality. That is so important in how you can shape yourself into being an adult, in choosing different decisions in your future because if you have no personality, anyone that comes in your life,—family, friends, loved ones, enemies—can persuade you to do something that you were not destined to be in your life and you will never know who you are as a person.

Jennifer Bacon: That is so profound. It's so true. I think you very much covered it. What reflections do you have on becoming a Black woman in today's world? You have taken your seat at the table.

Blue: I have so much to say. We try to minimize this but becoming a Black woman in society today is hard. It's [being] beautiful, disrespectful, and self-possessed. I'll say that because each Black woman in her life from the beginning of time, and Black men as well, were enslaved mentally, physically, and emotionally.

Blue: To this day, it is still a very present issue. Now, Black women have hard times changing the narrative in this whole situation, even in their own homes. For example, Black women are built to be strong, mentally and physically. We should be able to endure motherhood mentally, everything. However, you tend to see some articles or different aspects of women coming out with PPD, Postpartum Depression, or PTSD. It's becoming more and more common, women who could see and take on the bearing of motherhood and just being a family and being that ground solid. I guess you could say a fence to that home. It is very hard. Black women, we have realized this in this day and time, and we're doing things to change that by saying, "It's not hard to ask for help now." I will say that. It is not hard to reach out your hand and say, "I'm not okay." The beautiful thing about being a Black woman, and even during that whole situation, is that we seek and we strive until our resources have been used up and we just keep on going. We keep on going. It's just our ethics of us as Black women, talents. It is a beautiful thing that we have. The beauty of us is unquestionable. However, you know our ways to other races can be disrespectful and vulgar. However, other races do pretend and try to mimic our ways of being a Black woman to say the least. It's just our self-possession allows us to uplift each other and tell each other, "Your Black is beautiful. Being a Black woman in this world can and will be beautiful. It shall be beautiful." So, us doing that, we have more women in Congress and first ladies and teachers and nurses, and we just want to continue to strive. That would be my main reflection on becoming a Black woman in this world today. We still got some work to do but we have changed so far as Black women. I'm sorry it just, it touches me so much. You know you hear stories. Oh my gosh. My grandmother, my ancestors, lived through this. I will be everything I can be to show them that we live on our legacy.

Jennifer Bacon: Please don't be sorry. That is such a beautiful thing. I literally just got chills. I had a little shiver there. I think that's so spot on, and so necessary. I love what you were saying about our resilience and our strength and our beauty and all that came before us and all that will be coming in front of us and that we also don't have to do everything on our own. We can ask for help and we cannot always be strong. So, to hear you share all of that and be brought to tears just even thinking about that and this connection, this web of glorious Black women, our ancestry, our African ancestors. I love that it's bringing you to tears because that's all the process. Right? That's part of the healing, that's part of the strength to be able to share that. You said that so beautifully.

Blue: It saddens me when younger girls in this generation don't really understand and don't really deeply understand how beautiful being Black is in today's society because of what they're enduring, and because of social media and because of just unnecessary literature just being thrown at them.

Jennifer Bacon: Absolutely. You know, when we had the Poetic 8, one of the things that we did was around naming, naming yourself, creating your own identity. You talked about self-possession. So, obviously with all that you were experiencing and this tremendous loss of your mom is how you created your pen name Blue. If you today at 31 could create your pen name at this stage, what would your pen name be?

Blue: It would be Daisy. I like that.

Jennifer Bacon: What's your connection with Daisy? I love it.

Blue: When you look at daisies, you look at a new beginning, a spring, a new blossom, a new life, a new chance to start over. I was Blue. Now, I'm blossoming. Now, I'm shining bright. So, that would be my new name.

I'm grateful that I was able to experience this with you. This is not a common thing to have or be able to do at any school, for that matter. I'm going to say any school but for a school that is predominantly Black, I thought that was a rare thing. Honestly, I love poetry but I have never shared my poetry. I wrote different books and all kinds of stuff. Just books and books and books of poetry. My father actually liked my poetry. So, I gave him a couple of books. Being able to do that, God spoke to me back then and told me to join and to do this for myself. I was so ecstatic. It was so much fun. It was so educational as well. So, I truly thank you for that opportunity because who knows how to cope or how to deal with it if I didn't have that opportunity to express myself not just in words and writing, but also being able to express myself to some people that understood and just felt the same way.

Jennifer Bacon: That makes my heart soar. So, thank you, thank you. My goodness, that just lifts my spirit.

References

Adisa, O. P. (2006). *Eros muse.* Africa World Press.
Algozzine, B., O'Shea, D.J., Obiakor, F.E. (2009). *Culturally responsive literacy instruction.* Corwin Press.
Angelou, M. (1994). *Phenomenal woman.* Random House Publishing.
Ayers, W., & Ford, P. (Eds.). (1996). *City kids city teachers.* The New Press.
Babich, B. E. (2006). *Words in blood, like flowers.* State University of New York Press.
Bachelard, G. (1994). *The poetics of space.* Beacon Press.
Bacon, J. N. (1997). Strong and sassy. In David, DuBois, & King [Eds.], *Phati'tude Literary Magazine, 1*(1), 86.
Bacon, J.N. (2009). *Culturally responsive poetry: The lived experience of African American adolescent girl poets.* ProQuest Information.
Bacon, J. N. (2011a). They walk gingerly. In David, Bacon, & Tucker [Eds.], *Phati'tude Literary Magazine, 2*(4), 205.
Bacon, J.N. (2011b). Culturally responsive poetry. *Journal of Poetry Therapy, 24*(1) 1–15.
Bacon, J. N. (2016). Using culturally responsive and inclusive poetry groups with diverse teens. *Florida Reading Journal, 51*(3) 18–27.
Bacon, J.N. (2017). Writing in solidarity: The lived experience of African American adolescent girls writing poetry. *Journal of Poetry Therapy. 31*(3) 1–14.
Bacon, J. N. (2022). Academic mothering: Black women mentors in higher education. In S. Cupid & A. D. Tomlin (Eds.), *Black experiences in higher education: Faculty, staff, and students* (pp. 165–178). Information Age Publishing.
Barnhart, R. K. (1995). *The Barnhart concise dictionary of etymology: The origins of American English words.* HarperResource.
Beech, C. (1999). *Poetic culture.* Northwestern University Press.
Bigner, J. J. (1994). *Parent-child relations: An introduction to parenting.* Macmillan.
Braxton, J. M. (Ed.). (1989). *Black women writing autobiography.* Temple University Press.
Carroll, R. (1997). *Sugar in the raw: Voices of young black girls in America.* Three Rivers Press.
Casey, E. S. (1993). *Getting back into place.* Indiana University Press.
Clifton, L. (2000). *Blessing the boats: New and selected poems 1988-2000.* BOA Editions Ltd.
Collins, P. H. (2000). *Black feminist thought: Knowledge, consciousness, and the power of empowerment.* Routledge.
Collins, P.H. & Bilge, S. (2016). *Intersectionality: Key concepts.* Polity.

Crenshaw, K. (2005). Mapping the Margins: Intersectionality, Identity Politics, and Violence against Women of Color (1994). In R. K. Bergen, J. L. Edleson, & C. M. Renzetti, *Violence against women: Classic papers* (pp. 282–313). Pearson Education New Zealand.

Crenshaw, K. (2016). The urgency of intersectionality. TEDWomen.

Dance, L. J. (2002). *Tough fronts: The impact of street culture on schooling.* RoutledgeFalmer.

Dean, A.V., Salend, S.J., & Taylor, L. (1993). Multicultural education: A challenge for special educators. *Teaching Exceptional Children, 26*(1), 40–43

DeDonato, C. (Ed.). (2004). *City of one: Young writers speak to the world.* Aunt Lute Books.

Delpit, L., & Dowdy, J. K. (2002). *The skin that we speak: Thoughts on language and culture in the classroom.* The New Press.

Ferguson, A. A. (2001). *Bad boys: Public schools in the making of black masculinity.* University of Michigan Press.

Franco, B. (2001). *Things I have to tell you.* Candlewick Press.

Freire, P. (1994). *Pedagogy of hope* (R.R. Barr, Trans). Continuum.

Freire, P. (2000). *Pedagogy of the oppressed* (M.B. Ramos, Trans.). Continuum International Publishing Group. (original work published 1970)

Gadamer, H-G. (2004). *Truth and method* (J. Weinsheimer & D.G. Marshall, Trans.). Continuum. (original work published 1960)

Garran, C. S. (2004). *Encountering faces of the other: A phenomenological study of American high school students journeying through South Africa.* Unpublished doctoral dissertation, The University of Maryland, College Park.

Gibran, K. (1996). *The prophet.* Alfred A Knopf.

Gilbert, D. I. M. (Ed.). (1998). *Catch the fire: A cross-generational anthology of contemporary African-American poetry.* Riverhead Books.

Gilbert, E. (2006). *Eat, pray, love.* Penguin Books.

Gorman, J. C. (1999). Understanding children's hearts and minds: Emotional functioning and learning disabilities. *Teaching Exceptional Children, 31*(3), 72–77.

Graham, M. (1997). *On being female, black, and free: Essays by Margaret Walker: 1932–1992.* The University of Tennessee Press.

Hale, T. A. (1998). *Griots and griottes.* Indiana University Press.

Hamilton, E. (1969). *Mythology.* New York: Little, Brown and Company.

Hamilton, E. (1994). *What is now unanswerable: Poems.* Warrior Poets Press.

Heidegger, M. (1962). *Being and time* (J. Macquarrie & E. Robinson, Trans.). Harper & Row.

Heidegger, M. (1969). *The Essence of Reasons.* T. Malick (Trans.). Northwestern University Press.

Heidegger, M. (1971). *Poetry, language, thought* (A. Hofstadter, Trans.). HarperCollins.

Hilliard, A. G. (1998). *SBA: The reawakening of the African mind.* Makare.

Hilliard, A. G. (2002). *African power.* Makare.
Hlongwane, K. A., Ndlovu, S., & Mutloatse, M. (2006). *Soweto '76: Reflections of the liberation struggles.* Houghton.
Holy Bible. (1984). Holy Bible International Bible Society. Zondervan.
hooks, b. (1994). *Teaching to transgress.* Routledge.
Hull, G. T., Scott, P. B., & Smith, B. (Eds.). (1982). *All the women are white, all the blacks are men, but some of us are brave.* The Feminist Press.
Hultgren, F. (1995). The phenomenology of "doing" phenomenology: The experience of teaching and learning together. *Human Studies, 18,* 371–388.
Hurston, Z. (1942). *Dust tracks on a road.* HarperCollins.
Hynes, A. M., & Hynes-Berry, M. (1994). *Biblio/poetry therapy.* North Star Press.
Irvine, J. J. (2003). *Educating teachers for diversity: Seeing with a cultural eye.* Teachers College Press.
Jones, M. L. (1996). *The color of culture II.* Impact Communications.
Kauffmann, J. J. (1999). How we prevent the prevention of emotional and behavioral disorders. *Exceptional Children, 65,* 448–486.
Krell, D. F. (1993). *Martin Heidegger: Basic writings.*: HarperCollins.
Kunjufu, J. (n.d.). *Countering the conspiracy to destroy black boys* (Vol. III). African American Images.
Ladson-Billings, G. (1994). *The dreamkeepers.* Jossey-Bass.
Ladson-Billings, G. (1995). But that's just good teaching! The case for culturally relevant pedagogy. *Theory Into Practice, 34*(3), 159–165.
Lemons, G. L. (2008). *Black male outsider.* State University of New York Press.
Levin. D.M. (1985). *The body's recollection of being.* Routledge.
Levin, D. M. (1989). *The listening self.* Routledge.
Lincoln, A. (1966) Who will revere the black woman. *Negro Digest.* Retrieved online.
Lincoln, A. (2005). *The black woman.* Washington Square Press.
Lorde, A. (1997). *The collected poems of Audre Lorde.* W.W. Norton.
Lorde, A. (2007). *Sister outsider.* Crossing Press.
Love, B. (2019). *We want to do more than survive: Abolitionist teaching and the pursuit of educational freedom.* Beacon Press.
Lynn, M., Bacon, J. N., Totten, T., Bridges, T., & Jennings, M. (2010). Examining teachers' beliefs about African American students in a low-performing high school: The impact on African American males. *Teachers College Record, 112*(1).
Maloney, G. A. (1981). *Prayer of the heart.* Ave Maria Press.
Mama, A. (1995). *Beyond the masks: Race, gender and subjectivity.* Routledge.
Moyers, B. (1995). *The language of life.* Broadway Books.
Moran, D. (2000). *Introduction to phenomenology.* Routledge.
Morrison, T. (1973). *Sula.* Alfred A Knopf.
Morrison, T. (1987). *Beloved.* Penguin Books.

Morrison, T. (1994). *The bluest eye.* Penguin Books. (Original work published 1970)
Muhammad, G. (2023). *Unearthing joy: A guide to culturally and historically responsive teaching and learning.* Scholastic.
Nietzsche, F. (2006). *Nietzsche: On the Genealogy of Morality and Other Writings.* In the History of Political Thought (K. Ansell-Pearson, Ed.; C. Diethe, Trans.). Cambridge: Cambridge University Press.
O'Donohue, J. (1997). *Anam cara.* HarperCollins.
Oliver, M. (1986). *Dream work.* Atlantic Monthly Press.
Pizer, M. (1992). *Poems for comfort and healing.* Smithmark.
Richie, B. E. (1996). *Compelled to crime: The gender entrapment of battered black women.* Routledge.
Rilke, M. R. (2005). *Letters on life.* Random House.
Rilke, M. R. (1962). *Letters to a young poet.* W.W. Norton.
Risser, J. (1997). *Hermeneutics and the voice of the other.* State University of New York Press.
Rothstein, S. W. (1993). *The voice of the other: Language as illusion in the formation of the self.* Praeger.
Russell, M. (1982). Black-eyed blues connection: Teaching black women. In Hull, G. T., Scott, P. B., & Smith, B. (Eds.), *All the women are white, all the blacks are men, but some of us are brave* (pp. 196-207). The Feminist Press.
Safranski, R. (1998). *Martin Heidegger: Between good and evil.* Harvard University Press.
Schutz, S. P. (2001). *One world one heart.* Blue Mountain Press.
Sewell, M. (Ed.). (2006). *Growing up girl: An anthology from marginalized spaces.* Girlchild Press.
Sewell, M. (Ed.). (2008). *Just like a girl.* Girlchild Press.
Shange, N. (1997). *For colored girls who have considered suicide when the rainbow is enuf.* Scribner Poetry.
Sheftall, B.G. (Ed.). (1995). *Words of fire: An anthology of African American feminist thought.* The New Press.
Smith, B. (1998). *The truth that never hurts.* Rutgers University Press.
Smoley, R. (2002). *Inner Christianity.* Shambhala.
Spangler, A. (2004). *Praying the names of god.* Zondervan.
Steiner, G. (1989). *Real presences.* The University of Chicago Press.
Tolman, D. (1994). Doing desire: Adolescent girls' struggles for/with sexuality. *Gender and Society, 8*(3), 324–342.
Tolman, D. (1996). *Adolescent girls' sexuality: Debunking the myth of the urban girl.* NYU Press.
Turner, J. S., & Helms, D. B. (1991). *Lifespan development.* Holt, Rinehart and Winston.
van Manen, M., & Levering, B. (1996). *Childhood's secrets.* Teachers College Press.
van Manen, M. (1997). *Researching lived experience.* The Althouse Press.

van Manen, M. (2003). *Writing in the dark: Phenomenological studies in interpretive inquiry.* The Althouse Press.

Vendler, H. (Ed.). (1998). *T.S. Eliot the wasteland and other poems.* Signet Classic Penguin Group.

Walker, A. (2012). *Anything we love can be saved: A writer's activism.* Random House.

Walker, A. (2003). *In search of our mother's garden.* Mariner Books.

Walker, A. (2006). *We are the ones we have been waiting for: Inner light in a time of darkness.* The New Press.

Walsch, N. D. (1995). *Conversations with God: An uncommon dialogue book 1.* Penguin Putnam.

Walsch, N.D. (1997). *Conversations with God: An uncommon dialogue book 2.* Penguin Putnam.

Warch, W. (1977). *The new thought Christian.* DeVoross.

Weis, L., & Fine, M. (2000). Construction sites: An introduction. In L. Weis & M. Fine (Eds.), Construction sites: Excavating race, class and gender among urban youth (pp. xi–xiv). Teachers' College Press.

Welwood, J. (n.d.) Quote retrieved from https://www.azquotes.com/quote/893318

White, E. C. (1995). *Chain chain change: For black women in abusive relationships.* Seal Press.

White-Hood, M. (1989). *Safe in the heart of another: An ontological place to experience adolescence.* Unpublished dissertation, University of Maryland.

Wiseman, A. M. (2004). *Poetic connections: Using literacy to connect the classroom, community, and culture of middle school students.* ProQuest Information.

Williams, T. M. (2008). *Black pain.* Scribner.

Woodward, E. (1987). *Poets, prophets & pragmatists: A new challenge to religious life.* Ave Maria Press

Writerscorps. (Eds.). (2003). *Paint me like I am.* HarperCollins.

Wurtzel, E. (1998). *Bitch: In praise of difficult women.* Anchor Books.

X, M., & Haley, A. (1965). *The autobiography of Malcolm X.* Random House.

Zinn, M. B., & Dill, B. T. (1996). Theorizing difference from multiracial feminism. *Feminist Studies, 22*(2), 321–331.

Index

Activism vi, vii, 14, 31, 43, 44, 45, 54, 84, 115, 124, 138, 141, 146

Age compression 17

Ancestors 20, 26, 37, 41, 53

Bachelard, G. 4, 167

Black Feminism v, 7,8, 22, 29, 33, 41, 44, 45, 56, 70, 121, 125, 144, 148, 149, 150, 151, 154
Black Feminist Epistemology 70

Black male outsider 124, 125
I Am not a Man 124, 125, 126, 127, 128, 129, 130

Blue 54, 55, 56, 61, 62, 64-65, 66, 68, 69, 75, 82, 83, 85, 86, 87, 99, 101-102, 104, 105, 108, 118-119, 120, 127, 128, 129, 130, 133, 135-136, 137, 160-166

Clifton, L. 20, 37, 167

Collins, P.H. 43, 91, 167

Counter-narratives/counter-stories 6, 8, 22, 31

Crenshaw, K. 7, 30, 123, 168

Culturally Responsive Poetry v, 8, 22, 89, 90, 140, 141, 146, 147, 148, 149, 150, 156

Culturally responsive pedagogy 33, 42, 44, 138, 140, 143, 144, 149, 150

Ladson-Billings, G 42, 43, 44

Irvine. J.J. 42, 43, 44

Death 58, 61, 63, 64, 66, 68, 73

Heidegger, M. 45, 84, 134, 137, 157

Hermeneutics 50, 137

Hegemony 45, 68, 73

Hilliard, A. 41,

Home
  Homecoming; Homesteading 16,20, 21, 32, 33,35, 38, 39, 40, 41, 46, 47, 53, 55, 56. 60, 61, 63, 64, 71, 72, 73, 77, 78, 89, 90, 91, 92, 93, 94, 95, 101, 129, 132, 133, 134, 139, 140, 151, 152, 155

Hurston, Z.N. 54, 55, 57, 66

Keisha 18, 46, 76, 77, 78, 121, 159

Gadamer, H-G. 154

Grief 56, 58, 61, 68, 73, 82, 96

Griots and Griottes 41, 44, 46, 51

I Am 31, 50, 80, 92, 93, 97, 99, 104. 134, 145

Intersectionality v, vi, 6, 7, 8, 29, 123

Joy 24, 35, 38, 39, 42, 44, 55, 58, 60, 78, 92, 98, 106, 107, 134, 135, 137, 138, 139, 154, 156, 157

Muhammad, G. 44, 170

Poetic Eight 51-54, 62, 63, 64, 72, 73, 74, 75, 76, 78, 82, 85, 89, 93, 95, 98, 99, 102, 103, 106, 107, 110, 111, 112, 115, 118, 120, 121, 130. 132, 133, 134, 137, 138, 143, 154, 155, 157

Phenomenology 29, 32, 33, 45, 84, 89, 134, 152

Liberation/emancipation 22, 58, 84, 93, 94, 123, 125, 131

Living Words 27, 36, 134

Love 101, 102, 104, 105, 106, 109, 130, 132, 133, 134

Love, B. 30, 169

Lorde, A. 41, 110

Mishaps 54, 55, 56, 57, 61, 62, 64, 75, 88, 89, 96, 99, 108, 112, 113, 119-120, 134-135,

Motherhood 16, 23, 59, 60, 72, 86, 93, 97, 117, 135

Motherless Daughters 56, 59, 60

Morrison, T. 17, 54-56, 59, 61

My Girls 20, 21, 54, 126

Multiracial feminism 6, 7, 171

Naming 129

Racial disparities 6,

Sexuality 7, 11-13,

Silence 24, 154
  Epistemological silence 35
  Ontological silence 35
  Poetic silence 34
  Silence and voice 33, 153
  Silenced bodies 115
  Shame and Silence 116

Strong and Sassy 108, 110, 112, 115, 145

Strong Black Women 67, 69, 71, 72, 73, 81, 108, 115, 117

Suffocation 54, 62, 73, 96

Van Manen, M. 34, 35

Walker, A. 31, 32, 41, 63, 74, 116, 117, 157

What African American Adolescent Girls Do 29, 30

Author Bio

Dr. Jennifer Bacon is Core Doctoral Faculty in Human and Organizational Development at Fielding Graduate University. She earned her PhD in Curriculum and Instruction from the University of Maryland, College Park, and her MEd in Special Education from the University of Virginia. In addition to her extensive experience in education, she is an interfaith minister who is trained in the use of poetry therapy, spiritual guidance, and yoga. Deeply committed to addressing issues of racial and gender equity, overrepresentation in special education, and writing for transformation, social justice, creative expression, and healing, she participates in a number of professional associations, mentoring organizations, writing projects, and research work.

She has authored numerous articles and book chapters including, "Writing in Solidarity: The Lived Experience of African American Adolescent Girls Writing Poetry," "Using Culturally and Inclusive Poetry Groups with Diverse Teens," "Academic Mothering: Black Women Mentors in Higher Education," and "Examining Teachers' Beliefs About African American Male Students in a Low-Performing High School in an African American School District."

She is the author of *Sisters in the Dissertation House: A Dissertation Narrative*, which addresses doctoral completion by women of color in underrepresented fields. Her children's book titled, *I Am an Antiracist Superhero: With Activities to Help You Be One Too!* was released by Bala Kids in September of 2023.

www.ingramcontent.com/pod-product-compliance
Lightning Source LLC
Chambersburg PA
CBHW070358240426
43671CB00013BA/2546